HOW TO CUT DOWN YOUR SOCIAL DRINKING

HOW TO CUT DOWN YOUR SOCIAL DRINKING

by Richard A. Basini
with Peter Oliver

G. P. Putnam's Sons
New York

G. P. Putnam's Sons
Publishers Since 1838
200 Madison Avenue
New York, NY 10016

Copyright © 1985 by Richard A. Basini
All rights reserved. This book, or parts thereof,
may not be reproduced in any form without permission.
Published simultaneously in Canada by
General Publishing Co. Limited, Toronto

Library of Congress Cataloging in Publication Data

Basini, Richard.
  How to cut down your social drinking.

  1. Drinking of alcoholic beverages—United States.
2. Drinking of alcoholic beverages—Social aspects—
United States.   3. Entertaining—United States.
I. Oliver, Peter B.   II. Title.
HV5292.B37   1985   613.8′1   85-16747
ISBN 0-399-13109-4

Book Design by Constance Sohodski

Printed in the United States of America

1 2 3 4 5 6 7 8 9 10

CONTENTS

Foreword by Angier Biddle Duke	9
Winners and Losers	11
Typical Social Drinkers: Where Do You Fit In?	17
The Bottom Line: What You Give Up and What You Get	25
Setting Up a Program That Works for You	29
Four Basic Social-Drinking Situations: Know the Difference	29

The Proper Mental Approach: Don't Play Those Mind Games	32
Having a Plan—and Sticking with It	35
Developing Your Personal Drink-Reduction Program	37
Five Steps to Drink Reduction	40
Putting Your Plan into Action	45

Cocktail Parties 47
    Tips for Cutting Down 47
    A Note About Drinking at Office Parties 59

Dinners and Lunches 61
    The Inevitable Pressures and Temptations 61
    Tips for Cutting Down 64
    A Note About Doing Business and Staying Sober 76

Entertaining at Home 79
    What's Your Responsibility? 79
    Tips for Cutting Down 82

Tips That Work Anytime 93

Make a Game of It 107

A Few Personal Notes 109

Send in Your Tips 113

An Important Note

This book is for social drinkers who are seeking an effective way to keep their drinking within moderate levels. It is for people who have the ability to control their drinking if they so choose. It is *not* for people with serious drinking problems. There is no such thing as "drinking in moderation" for the alcoholic. Alcoholism is a disease. People with serious drinking problems should be encouraged to seek professional consultation and treatment.

FOREWORD
by Angier Biddle Duke

We are entering a new age now, of more understanding in regard to social drinking. I do not believe that the pressures to drink are as insistent or persistent as they have been in the past. The new attitudes and policies toward smoking have also encouraged a reevaluation of society's sense of conformity about the use of alcoholic beverages. A diet cola is now virtually a status symbol at social events, and its drinker attracts more positive than negative reactions.

All of which means that now perhaps more than ever we have the opportunity to limit our drinking to the level we ourselves choose. This is why Richard Basini's book is so timely. At this moment of easing attitudes and new possibilities for personal choice, he provides a bounty of very practical suggestions in a sane, systematic, and thoroughly appealing way. If I were to give anyone advice on survival in this still very wet world of ours, I would certainly employ his wise counsel.

Angier Biddle Duke was chief of protocol of the White House and the Department of State during the Kennedy and Johnson administrations and has served as United States ambassador to four nations. He is now the chairman of the United States–Japan Foundation.

WINNERS AND LOSERS

After a long series of phone calls, I had finally arranged a lunch date with the key man in charge of a potentially lucrative account. Landing the account would mean nearly doubling my total billings. So I put in hours of careful preparation. I worked up a presentation that I knew would knock his socks off—with charts, schedules, and a complete campaign mapped out from A to Z.

As we sat down at the restaurant, he invited me to have a drink, and I accepted. When he ordered us a second round, I wanted to object but didn't feel I could. By the time we were halfway through the meal—and halfway through a bottle of wine—the time had come for me to make my presentation.

But I never opened my briefcase. My presentation demanded clear, logical thinking. I knew I had to be on my toes to make it work. But I'd lost my edge.

How to Cut Down Your Social Drinking

I could have kicked myself. In that situation, did I really have no choice but to accept a second drink? Did I really have to share in the wine? As I thought more about it, I realized how easily I fell into the same kind of trap in my social life as well. When offered a refill at a party, it was always easier to say yes. And yet those extra drinks did little for me but increase the bulk around my waistline and decrease my alertness at the office the next day.

I knew that I wasn't the only one who fell into that trap. A friend who is an architect told me that he felt obliged to have a couple of beers with the construction foreman each night in order to keep the project on target. One or two beers, he said, didn't hurt. Although he was beginning to look like some of the older workers around the middle, being "one of the guys" was something he felt he just had to do. When hard pressed, however, he conceded that Philip Johnson and I. M. Pei probably didn't do business that way.

A female client of mine confessed that she saw drinking as a built-in part of her job. Her work required her to attend a number of business-related social functions where drinks were usually served. She felt she always had to be ready to join in. Yet her boss seemed able to duck those drinks effortlessly.

A friend who is a lawyer insisted that he had to have "a couple of pops" after a long day in court to relieve the intense pressure. But I could see that he was just a step away from real trouble. He was worried that he might not make partner in his firm. And those drinks were beginning to get in the way of his family life. I left him at the bar as he was having one more drink before heading home.

Then I looked at the other side of the coin. As the head of a public relations agency, I do business daily with highly successful people who have more demanding business and social schedules than most. Yet these superachievers manage to survive the myriad receptions, dinner parties, and special events they are obliged to attend and come away looking fresh and trim.

Why are some people able to have complete control over their social drinking, whereas others find the pressure to drink stronger than their resistance? How is it that some of us—by choice, out of sense of duty, or for reasons we aren't even sure of—end up drinking more than we really want?

I made up my mind to find out. I decided to find out how the superachievers keep their alcoholic intake under control and still have as good a time as anyone else. I started asking around, calling friends, keeping my eyes and ears open, collecting ideas from people who know how to keep their social drinking under control.

What I discovered in the process was that:

- I am not alone. Virtually everyone I spoke with either had a method or was looking for a method to avoid extra, unwanted drinks.

- You can easily and painlessly cut at least four or five drinks from your weekly intake.

- Most important: *Successful people don't drink much. Period.*

I can say now, without hesitation, that the level of a person's success is inversely proportional to the amount he or she drinks. The person who has two or three drinks a week won't necessarily be significantly less successful than the absolute teetotaler.

However, the person who knocks back half a dozen drinks a day has absolutely no chance of achieving his or her full potential. It's as simple as that.

For people who value their time, a hangover is a useless and expensive luxury. When they drink less, they can make more constructive use of their time at social functions. As the imbibers tell one another jokes and exchange slaps on the back, the more successful people are getting something useful out of each social encounter.

Armed with these observations, I decided to put what I had learned into a book—a book for social drinkers who have trouble avoiding drinks they really don't want. It is a book for those who want to drink more sensibly without missing out on the fun. It is for people who want to enjoy an occasional drink and still be able to conduct business in a clear-headed, professional manner.

This book will offer you specific tips from successful people to help you keep your drinking at a level *you* feel good about. You'll learn how to plan your drinking in advance, how to drink less so that every drink is a treat. You'll learn to take control over just how many drinks you have on a daily, weekly, and monthly basis. You'll learn that you can plan your social drinking in the same way you plan your vacation, your diet, or your monthly budget.

I personally have discovered that the benefits of cutting back are real and rewarding. The most noticeable, of course, is that I was able to lose ten pounds in the first four months and am steadily making progress toward a slimmer waistline. The calories from drinking (and munching while drinking) won't be missed. And avoiding a couple of drinks and hors d'oeuvres at a cocktail party is like cutting out an entire meal's worth of calories.

Winners and Losers

I also feel better. That's sometimes hard to define, but I know that my head is always clear in the morning, and I've been getting to work earlier and accomplishing more than ever before.

Most important, I've found a wealth of time for other activities in my life. The time I used to spend with friends or clients "over cocktails" has translated itself into accomplishing creative ventures that I once complained "I just don't have time for." I have that time now.

In short, I have found that controlled social drinking is a giant step toward success, both in my business and my personal life. I hope you'll join me in taking that step.

TYPICAL SOCIAL DRINKERS
Where Do You Fit In?

Meet Joe, a super guy with a great sense of humor and lots of friends—and a fondness for liquor. Joe is the sort who never intends to have more than three drinks at a social occasion or a business get-together. Sometimes he succeeds, but when he's having a really good time (and that's what usually happens) he ends up drinking more—and often regretting it the next day. Joe may not have a "drinking problem," but most people would agree that he drinks pretty heavily. Most people would also agree that he's a social drinker.

Now meet Anne, a woman in her mid-thirties who has just started her own retail clothing business. She often has a glass of wine or two at a business lunch, and after a particularly hectic workday, she may have a drink when she gets home, to unwind. She drinks nowhere near as much as Joe, but she, too, would be considered a social drinker.

How to Cut Down Your Social Drinking

Therein lies problem number one. Such is the looseness of our language that the term "social drinker" applies with equal accuracy to the person who has an occasional drink or two, like Anne, and the person like Joe who may have as many as four or five drinks a day. Essentially, a social drinker is anyone between the absolute teetotaler and the heavy drinker—the person who enjoys having a drink at a social occasion or a drink in the evening to relax.

Problem number two: Not everyone has the same tolerance for alcohol, nor does alcohol produce the same effects for every person. Two glasses of wine for lunch may make Anne a little woozy. Joe, on the other hand, may be able to down four martinis after work before being slowed down by his liquor consumption. In fact, Joe may be one of those guys who rather foolishly prides himself on being able to gulp down copious amounts of liquor without showing the effects of it.

Surely you've seen the charts showing how many drinks you should be able to consume, given your weight, before you are legally drunk. Helpful, maybe—but in the end, you are the final judge of how much you can drink without producing unwanted side effects. The level of alcohol in your blood may be well below the legal limit, but if you're feeling light-headed and loose-tongued while you're drinking, and you suffer the consequences later, you can consider yourself as having reached (or exceeded) your personal limit.

To get you started, here are a few definitions, so you know exactly whom we're talking about. For the purposes of this book, let's divide drinkers into three categories:

- *Alcoholics.* People with a physical addiction to alcohol. Alcoholism is a disease. The body's chemical balance has become thrown out of kilter in order to accommodate a physical craving for alcohol. It is possible to be an alcoholic without being a heavy drinker, although obviously the two usually go together.

• **Heavy drinkers.** A heavy drinker is someone who drinks a lot, drinks regularly, and can't keep his or her drinking under reasonable control. Drinking is probably causing problems at home or at work.

• **Social drinkers.** This includes everyone else who drinks—rarely, occasionally, or on a regular basis. A heavy social drinker differs from a heavy drinker in that drinking hasn't yet become a psychological dependence and is causing no serious personal or emotional problems. However, if you're putting down twenty-five or more drinks a week (and though you may think you don't, wait until you start counting), you're probably headed in that direction. But you can still control your drinking and can cut down to more moderate consumption levels if you choose to.

This book is for social drinkers *only*. It's for people who, for a variety of reasons, may end up drinking more than they like:

• because they enjoy drinking and find it hard to turn down the pleasure of a drink when it's offered.

• because they have a heavy schedule of social engagements at which drinks are usually considered a part of the occasion.

• because they encounter situations in which they feel pressured to drink even when they don't want to.

In short, this book is for people who want to and can cut down on the amount they drink and still get the kind of pleasure they are looking for from drinking.

How to Cut Down Your Social Drinking

Where You Stand

Look at the chart on the following two pages to find out where you stand among social drinkers. Your objective in using this book isn't necessarily to get you to the top of the ladder or even to get you to abstain altogether. Instead, the idea is to help you move up on the chart until you arrive at a level of drinking you feel good about. It might be helpful to note that the generally accepted definition of moderate drinking is two two-ounce drinks a day. (Beer and wine, of course, count too.) Ideally, you should want to position yourself at one of the levels between light and moderate.

Don't kid yourself about the amount you drink. Be honest. Make a candid attempt to determine what your *typical* consumption pattern is. Example: You usually have two drinks in the evening when you get home. On the average, you usually have three lunch meetings a week, and you usually have a drink at each. Four evenings a week you stay home and have two drinks before you dine. Three times a week you entertain or are entertained. At such functions you tend to have three drinks. Add them all up:

```
Drinks at lunch ....................................... 3
Drinks at home (4 nights)............................. 8
Drinks at social occasions ............................ 9
                                             total  20
```

Typical Social Drinkers

Obviously, the number you come up with at first will be an estimate. It doesn't have to be exact, but be as precise as you can. Once you start taking control of the amount you drink, and you start counting each drink, your typical weekly consumption will be much easier to determine.

TYPICAL SOCIAL DRINKERS

Social Drinking Level	Type of Social Drinker	Average Weekly Consumption*
I	Light	Fewer than 6 drinks
II	Light to moderate	6 to 11 drinks
III	Moderate (type A)	12 to 17 drinks
IV	Moderate (type B)	12 to 17 drinks
V	Moderate to heavy (type A)	18 to 24 drinks
VI	Moderate to heavy (type B)	18 to 24 drinks
VII	Heavy	25 or more drinks
VIII	Heavy	30 or more drinks

*A drink is one 2-ounce mixed drink, a glass of wine, or a 12-ounce bottle of beer.

TYPICAL SOCIAL DRINKERS

Typical Pattern of Consumption	Comments
You have an occasional drink at social get-togethers.	No problem—except that sometimes you feel pressured to drink when you don't want to.
You don't drink regularly but you enjoy a drink when friends get together.	You should make sure you don't overdo it when the party is really going strong.
You usually have two drinks a day, generally in the evening. You rarely have more than three.	You're a fairly typical social drinker. You know when to stop. You could drink less if you wanted.
You usually have one or two drinks a day, but sometimes have three and then lose control.	No problems with two drinks or fewer. Your first objective is to stick to a two-drink limit.
You're a frequent drinker, pretty good at limiting yourself to three drinks at social functions.	Your drinking is locked in a regular pattern. Your first objective is to break your routine.
You're a frequent drinker who tends to have a little too much at social functions.	Your drinking is under control—most of the time. But watch out when party time rolls around.
You have two or three cocktails every evening, often two at lunch. You tend to overdo it at social functions.	You're a potential problem drinker. You should have no problem trimming five to six drinks from your weekly consumption.
You drink regularly and often, both at lunch and in the evening. You typically consume four or more drinks a day.	Time to cut your consumption. You are on your way to a drinking problem.

THE BOTTOM LINE:
What You Give Up and What You Get

Why give up that extra drink at a cocktail party, the martini at lunch, the second glass of wine at dinner? After all, it tastes and feels terrific. Yet the allure of an extra drink often cleverly obscures the benefits you stand to gain by saying no. Such benefits as:

• **Losing weight.** A martini, with 150 to 200 calories, is about the caloric equivalent of a nice, juicy lamb chop. Just imagine stuffing down two or three lamb chops before your lunch or dinner. Actually, with the lamb chops, you'd at least be getting some nutritional value. The calories in liquor are what doctors call "empty" calories—that is, calories that are accompanied by virtually no nutrients. Having a drink isn't a whole lot different from spooning down straight sugar.

Also, moderate consumption of alcohol usually acts as an appetite stimulant. By drinking less, you'll be less tempted to dig into a big heavy meal. And you probably won't casually toss down hundreds of calories worth of peanuts, crackers, and cheese.

- **Having more fun at parties.** No question about it—a drink or two can help loosen you up, particularly at a party where you don't know many people. When you feel a little more relaxed—and a couple of drinks certainly have a relaxing effect—you have a better time.

It's not too hard to get too much of a good thing, of course. After the first drink or two, the socializing benefits of drinking drop off rapidly. You become less alert and less aware of the people around you. Your sense of humor loses its sharpness, although you may not think so at the time. Your memory gets a little hazy. You say things you don't mean to. And so on. You recognize the symptoms.

The catch-22 is that drinking more can make you *feel* as if you are having a better time. Part of liquor's toxic effect is that it creates a delusory sense of confidence and well-being.

So why fool yourself? By limiting the amount you drink, you can still get the benefits of drinking—the relaxation and good feeling associated with liquor. At least half of the relaxing effect of having a drink is simply having something to do with your hands. So get a drink and sip it slowly. You might want to refill it with something nonalcoholic. You'll find yourself getting more involved with the people and the conversation around you. And you'll probably find that other people are more interested in you, too. Put yourself in the other person's shoes for the moment: It can get pretty annoying trying to make conversation with someone who is fumbling around with his or her words or memory.

- **Feeling healthier.** It is a medical fact that heavy drinking can bring on a stream of long-term consequences, everything from gastric problems to cancer. However, certain medical studies have shown that light to moderate amounts of alcohol can actually be good for you—helping you relax and producing some cardiovascular benefits while having minimal negative impact on your health. Most doctors agree that about four ounces of liquor a day—roughly two drinks—is the point at which more drinking begins to tip the scale toward negative health consequences.

Your body sends out signals of its own to report to you that you may be having more than is good for you. The most obvious (and oppressive) is a hangover the next morning. You may also become dehydrated, have skin problems, memory loss, and so on.

By drinking less, you'll not only feel healthier but look healthier. Your eyes and skin will take on a better color. People will notice, too.

In addition, overindulgence can induce a feeling of lethargy, as can moderate to heavy drinking on a regular basis. By drinking less, you'll feel more energetic. You may feel uncomfortable at first with that renewed energy, but you'll appreciate it when you come up with a way of putting it into action.

- ***Being more productive at work.*** Certainly one good place to put that newfound energy to work is at the office. After a fun party the night before where you couldn't resist raising a glass for one reason or another, you've probably experienced a feeling of listlessness the next day at work. When you raised a glass several times too often, you may have spent most of the morning simply trying to keep your head up and your eyes focused. No need for that. It takes time for alcohol to work its way through your system. A rough yardstick is that it takes at least an hour for your body to metabolize each drink. However, that doesn't mean you'll be fully recovered eight hours later if you have eight drinks. Better to have just a drink or two, enjoy the party, and be ready to go first thing the following morning.

• **Saving money.** The savings may seem modest until you start to add them up. Let's say that you cut back by one drink a day for the next year. And let's say that the average drink costs about $2. At that rate, you'll save $730 a year.

Obviously, you don't pay for every drink that you have. But by drinking just a little less, you can expect to save at least $500 a year. You can save even more if, when entertaining at home, you keep the flow of liquor to a reasonable level. It's not the beginning of a family fortune, but it is a healthy start of a little vacation fund.

• **Having a better sex life.** This is not a promise. Drinking less won't automatically improve your sex life. For the most part, it's up to you to make that happen. Even so, consider the facts: A sloppy drunk is *not* a turn-on—even an unsloppy drunk isn't especially sexy. Physiologically, too much drink can impair performance—*if* you can remember what to do when the moment of truth arrives. Finally, your spouse or lover is unlikely to be very sympathetic, and may be quite annoyed, when you're a moaning, hung-over dullard the next day.

You may discover a few peripheral benefits as well. For example, people who drink regularly often have cigarettes while they drink. Drinking and smoking are good friends. You may find it easier to cut down or stop smoking if you cut down on the amount you drink.

In short, by drinking a little less, you'll find yourself enjoying life more and being more productive. That's a pretty enticing opportunity.

SETTING UP A PROGRAM THAT WORKS FOR YOU

Four Basic Social-Drinking Situations: Know the Difference

You obviously shouldn't approach all social-drinking situations with the same attitude. If you do, you're looking for trouble—not just by drinking too much, but by risking a social or business gaffe that may have lasting repercussions.

There are some situations in which it's fine to have that extra drink. In other situations you'll need to be mentally alert and on your toes at all times.

Use the following breakdown as a guide:

How to Cut Down Your Social Drinking

• *Social.* Unquestionably, these occasions are the most enjoyable times to drink. This is the type of party among good friends who want to let their hair down, enjoy a drink or two, and have a fine time together. This is the kind of party at which you can tell an off-color joke, dance until midnight, wear a funny hat, and generally act pretty much as you please. Everybody knows you well, so your reputation isn't on the line. You don't have to worry about what people will think the next day. Occasions that are entirely social are also the times when you are most likely to overindulge.

• *Social Business.* This type of occasion is usually held at a club, a restaurant, someone's home, or some other nonbusiness location. Although this kind of function is intended primarily to be social, there are definite business overtones.

The idea is to have a good time, but there is usually an additional reason for this kind of party. It may be related to a political rally, an industry or business association function, or perhaps even admission to a club. It has all the appropriate social trappings, but don't be fooled. People are looking you over. You might run into the president of your company or the chairman of the board. Have a drink, even two, but drink only the amount you are fully confident you can handle. Be ready for business at any time.

• *Business Social.* This type of function is specifically designed either to further business associations or open new avenues of communication with people you might end up doing business with in the future. More formal (and often with an agenda more structured) than the social/business occasion, it allows for doing business in a setting more social and relaxed than the office.

And it works. Ask anyone who lives in Washington, D.C.,

Setting Up a Program That Works for You

where people will tell you that more business gets done at this type of "social" function than at official committee meetings or executive sessions. Your goal at this kind of occasion should be to take full advantage of business opportunities, not social opportunities. In other words: Keep your drinking to a minimum.

• *Business.* This particular type of function is *all* business. Take the example of the New York law firm with the tradition of having cocktails every Friday afternoon. Although it appears social enough, there's no mistaking this function for anything other than business. In this case, the partners may be on the lookout for those with social graces, or those who can handle themselves well under pressure. As a matter of protocol, you'll probably end up having a drink in this situation. But you'd be a fool to have more than that—especially at the end of the day on an empty stomach.

Your success as a social drinker depends on your ability to recognize beforehand what kind of situation you are going to encounter. As you develop ways to cut back on the amount you drink, you might want to choose priorities. If so, you'll be most productive by cutting back on drinking in those situations with more of a business bent. People who are successful professionals almost never drink at so-called "social" functions that are really business affairs.

The Proper Mental Approach: Don't Play Those Mind Games

To set the stage for bringing your drinking habits under control, it's important that you first establish the proper frame of mind.

Many times, having an extra drink is pretty much a part of a mindless process. You may be in the midst of a conversation and offer your glass to the host without thinking. Your glass may be refilled by the host or bartender without your even asking. Avoiding those traps is part of having a firm plan about your drinking. We'll talk more about that later.

But more often than not, having more to drink than you want starts well *before* having the first sip. It starts with a subconscious mental process, in which you rationalize that having a couple of drinks is okay.

Think of the things that little voice in the back of your head tells you before you set out for a cocktail party, dinner with friends, or other social occasion. Things like:

"You've had a tough day. You're tense and tired. You need a drink."

"You don't know anyone there. Having a drink will help you relax and meet people."

"If you have a drink with these people it might help you close the deal."

"This is a big occasion. All your friends are going to be there. You deserve to celebrate."

Setting Up a Program That Works for You

"These are a hard-drinking bunch of guys. You'd better be ready to hang right in there with them."

Any of these—and probably a dozen more that you can think of—is an understandable reason for wanting a drink. The only problem is: You're breaking down your resistance before you've even started. It's no wonder then that you find it easy to fall into the trap of having more to drink than you want.

In most social-drinking situations, you hardly need any added push to break down your resistance. The pressures or enticements to imbibe are usually built in, and after you've had a drink or two, much harder to resist. For example:

- Your good friend urges you to sit down over drinks and chat.

- Your partner from the office wants to discuss a little last-minute business. He wants you to have a drink because he's having one.

- The absolutely perfect host is always checking up on you when your glass is almost empty, or he's hired a crack team of waiters to make sure no one is without drink.

- This is an especially festive occasion when corks are popping and everyone seems to be raising a glass in celebration.

In short, there will be plenty of encouragement for you to drink in most social-drinking situations. So why look for a good reason to drink *before* heading toward the party?

What you should do instead is put yourself in a more sensible frame of mind. Although drinking may be a focal part of the occasion, nobody really throws a party and no one sets up a

How to Cut Down Your Social Drinking

social or business function just for people to come and drink. (If you know people who do, that's their problem. Obviously, you would never want to show up at that kind of event.) There is always another reason for an organized social occasion: a get-together of old friends, a theater or gallery opening, a charity dinner, and so on.

Before heading for the party, remind yourself of the reason the affair is being given and try to make the most of the occasion. If you're getting together with friends you haven't seen for a long time, really make a point of catching up on what they're doing. If it's a theater opening, follow the play closely, so you'll have something to talk about at the reception afterward and won't end up hanging around the bar with drink in hand.

Think of what you can contribute to the occasion, and also what you stand to gain from it. If you think you can contribute nothing and gain nothing, then there is no point in going. But at most occasions there is probably someone you'll want to see or meet, someone with whom you'd like to discuss important business matters. Social-business and business-social functions are great opportunities to make contacts or initiate business dealings in a relaxed atmosphere.

Whatever you do, don't look at the occasion as an opportunity to drink—even if it is called a "cocktail party." Cocktails are an attractive but very expendable part of the show—like balloons and cotton candy at the fair.

As Phyllis Diller, the well-known star, puts it so well: "We spend most of our lives trying to gain control, so it seems foolish to drink anything that leads to loss of control."

Setting Up a Program That Works for You

Having a Plan— and Sticking with It

A big part of establishing the proper mental approach about drinking beforehand is having a plan. Set up a specific strategy that's going to enable you to avoid the traps and the temptations that are built into most social-drinking situations.

That might sound like a quasi-militaristic approach, but you don't have to wear a gas mask to each social function just to make sure you won't take a sip! You're going to want to get as much enjoyment out of the party as everybody else. And you can. But with a little preparation, you can cut down on the amount you drink at the party—without giving up any of the fun.

So have a plan. Approach each social function with a clear idea of how much you want to drink and what you want to accomplish. Among other strategies that you will devise for yourself, your plan should include:

• *A specific number of drinks you intend to limit yourself to.* Be realistic. Part of the pleasure you'll get from reducing your drink consumption is a sense of accomplishment. Going over your limit by even one drink will make you feel as if you haven't achieved anything. So don't set too severe a goal initially.

• *A time limit for how long you intend to stay at the social function.* Obviously, you won't always be able to stay within the limit. You get caught in a conversation, your spouse wants to stay longer, or, at a formal occasion, ceremonies drag on a little longer than expected. And you don't want to be a dud who is always leaving the party before the fun really starts.

Even so, be as firm as you can about a time limit. At most cocktail parties or receptions, the liquor starts flowing more freely as the evening progresses. Obviously, if you stay later, you're running a greater risk of going over your preset drink limit.

• *A specific purpose (other than drinking!) for attending the function.* It may provide an opportunity to do a little business in a relaxed atmosphere. You may get a chance to make contact with a long-lost friend. If you can't come up with any good reason to go, then don't go. That should be simple enough.

• *A specific set of people you intend to do most of your mingling with.* Of course, at a small dinner party, or at a function where you know almost no one, that's going to be tough. But when you attend a party among friends or business associates, there are usually individuals or a group of people who drink more than the rest of the crowd. You don't have to avoid those people—they might be good friends. Just don't spend the whole evening with them.

Approaching social occasions with a drinking "game plan" will seem a little contrived. You may have problems at first keeping within your drink limit. But think of it as you would a diet or an exercise regimen. It's a matter of discipline—a difficult adjustment at first, but second nature after a while. And once you've successfully reduced your drinking to a level you feel satisfied with, don't be surprised if you find yourself adjusting your plan so that you can cut back even more. That's not unlike the lifetime armchair athlete who, to his amazement, after deciding to try running a mile or two, finds himself running forty miles a week. In the next chapter, we'll show you ways to incorporate your plan in weekly, monthly, and yearly programs. But you have to take the first step by finding out what kind of plan is going to get you started.

Setting up a plan sounds simple enough. All good ideas look good in theory. The hard part is putting them into action. That's what this book is really all about—tips, tricks, and suggestions that will help you stay within the limits you set for yourself. By putting the tips to work for you, you'll find that sticking to your plan isn't nearly as difficult as you might think.

Developing Your Personal Drink-Reduction Program

Now it's time to buckle down and get serious. Presumably you're expecting long-term results from your program. You don't just want to cut out a few drinks at the next cocktail party. You don't want to live the high life most of the time and cut back occasionally when you feel that you may be going too far.

You want a drink-reduction program that is going to last.

So how do you do that? First you have to lay the proper groundwork. You have to:

• **Be selective.** Don't try to put every tip in this book to work right away. You know yourself, the social-drinking occasions you usually encounter, and the types of pressures and temptations you have to endure. Within that context, select only the tips you think can really do the job for you. Keep it simple.

How to Cut Down Your Social Drinking

• ***Be consistent.*** If you have ever gone on a diet or participated in an exercise program, you're well aware of the kind of discipline it takes to avoid the occasional temptation or laziness when you first start. You're facing a tough challenge in shaking yourself from comfortable old patterns.

Yet in order to lose weight or get in shape, you have to stick with your program. There's no such thing as being on a diet 90 percent of the time.

The same is true of the program you devise for yourself to cut back on your social drinking. You can't seriously think of yourself as having made any progress if you cut your liquor consumption five days a week and then go crazy the other two. Doctors will tell you that it is more unhealthy to drink just one or two nights a week, but drink heavily, than it is to have two or three drinks every night. That occasional alcohol blast is real punishment for your body.

• ***Be patient.*** On the other side of the coin, you have to be patient with yourself, too. Expect a reasonable period of adjustment. The first two weeks that you start your drink-reduction program are likely to be marked by ups and downs—days when you stay well within your preset drink limit and days when you exceed it. Don't be too discouraged or give up easily just because you aren't an instant success. Keep working at it. If you are committed to keeping your drinking within moderate levels, moderate drinking will come naturally as you stick with your program. You are trying to create a new pattern or routine, and in doing so you may be fighting a routine that has been nurtured for many years.

• ***Be creative.*** The uniqueness of this program, unlike most diets or exercise programs, is that it is one *you devise yourself*. You might want to think of the tips in this book as your building

Setting Up a Program That Works for You

blocks, with you as the architect. Come up with a design that suits you. So if, for example, you try Tip #12 a dozen times and it has absolutely no impact on your liquor consumption, try another tip or strategy. Just because a tip works for someone else, that doesn't mean it will automatically be effective when you try it.

• **Be realistic.** Check back to the chart on pages 22–23. Again, determine where you stand on the social-drinking scale. (Remember, a drink is two ounces of liquor, a twelve-ounce beer, or a glass of wine.) Come up with your *typical* consumption pattern. Since you probably aren't in the habit of counting your drinks, it may mean a little guesswork. It may take a couple of weeks to determine your social-drinking level, and if so, you might want to make an early adjustment in your program.

When you first start out, set your target at *one level above your current level*. You will probably go farther after achieving that first goal. But if you are a heavy social drinker, don't think that you'll suddenly become a light drinker in a week. Well-grooved routines don't fade easily. Also, more severe reductions may produce withdrawal symptoms that can irritate you and your friends.

So set a goal that is realistic. If your typical weekly consumption is thirty drinks, cutting five or six drinks from the count can be done almost imperceptibly. After adjusting to that level, move on from there. Again, compare your program with a diet. If you've ever tried one of those lose-ten-pounds-in-a-week diets, you know it's easy to turn around and put those ten pounds back on in two weeks. Diets work best when weight comes off gradually, as you redefine your eating habits.

Five Steps to Drink Reduction

You can achieve significant gains toward your drink-reduction goal by following this five-step program. A reminder: The tips are your building blocks, and you can use them however and whenever you think they'll be most effective for you. This five-step program is the framework; you fill in the gaps.

Step 1
The Daily Plan

You should have a pretty good idea of your social agenda at the beginning of each day. Things may come up unexpectedly during the course of the day. If so, make an adjustment; don't let that unexpected call from a friend who wants to go out for drinks after work throw your whole schedule for a loop. If you find that you're going to have an extra drink you didn't think you'd have, cut a drink from another part of your schedule. The final daily tally is what you should be most concerned about.

So set up a chart for the day that will include:

- Your social schedule for the day
- The number of drinks you would normally consume

Setting Up a Program That Works for You

- The number of drinks you think you can *reasonably* limit yourself to.

Your chart should look like the one following page 114.

Remember: If you miss your target for one occasion, try to make up for it at another. Achieving your *daily* target is most important. And if your day is especially full of social engagements, adjust your target (within reason). If you have more than three social events on your schedule for the day, you should be looking for events where you can get away without drinking at all.

Writing down all that information may strike you as being a lot of work at first. But it is good reinforcement—a bit like signing a contract with yourself. After a while, the daily chart will probably become unnecessary. You'll have confidence in yourself and be more aware of how to handle each social occasion. But keep a daily record for the first month, or even two months—until you find that your awareness has become natural to you. It will provide a clear indication of the social-drinking situations in which you handle yourself well and those situations in which you need hard work to stay within your present limit. (In the back of this book you'll find blank forms that you can use. Feel free to photocopy them.)

Step 2
The Weekly Record

This is just an extension, really, of your daily plan. Because you'll be basing your drink consumption on the amount you consume each week, your final weekly tallies will be more valuable than your final daily tallies. Again, that doesn't mean you should abstain for most of the week and go overboard the rest.

Set up a weekly table, and keep it simple. Enter your figures from your daily charts. Once you decide you will no longer keep daily charts, enter the figures directly onto the weekly table the next day. And don't fudge the figures. If you had a double, that's two drinks, not one.

Your weekly record should look like the one in the section following page 114.

You may end up discarding your daily charts, but retain your weekly records for several months. That's the only way you're going to be able to track your progress and be prepared to make your monthly evaluations.

Step 3
The Monthly Evaluation

At the end of each month, compare your weekly records. Are you making progress toward the level of drinking you want to achieve? Remember, you're trying to track your typical, not necessarily your average, weekly consumption. You don't have to be absolutely precise, but be fair with yourself.

In calculating your progress, don't weigh extraordinary situations equally with a more typical day. For example, if you had a big night to celebrate a promotion (which is understandable), throw that night out. On the other end of the scale, if you were laid up for days with the flu and drank almost nothing, don't fool yourself into thinking you're making progress.

After two months, you should be well on your way to achieving your first goal—the next level up on the social drinkers chart. If you're not making much progress at that point, it's time either to crack down or change your plan. Be creative—choose tips that work for you.

If your weekly records indicate that you stay consistently within your target level, then it's time to move on to the next level. Begin the process all over again. Particularly for heavier social drinkers, moving to the next level will probably be more difficult than successfully achieving the first. So give yourself more time. However, at the three-or four-month point, you should be showing signs of progress. If not, crack down or change your plan.

When you arrive at the drinking level *you're happy with*, continue your weekly records and monthly evaluations for a while longer. The idea is not just to get to the level you want, but to *stay* there. Give yourself at least three months to be sure that you can stay comfortably at that social-drinking level.

Your chart should look like the one in the section following page 114.

Step 4
Keeping Track of the Benefits

Not all the benefits you'll get from drinking less are easily quantifiable. Did you get a raise because you were more productive at work, and were you more productive because you were drinking less? The connection may be there—and if so, make a note of it—but don't expect it and then become annoyed if it doesn't materialize.

However, you *can* keep track of the calories and the money

you'll save by cutting down. Make the calorie loss and the money saved a part of your reward.

Multiply each drink cut from your normal weekly consumption by 150 calories, the calories in an average drink. If you are able to cut your liquor consumption by a drink a day, you will have cut 4,200 calories from your monthly consumption. That is as if you fasted for almost two full days of the month!

Of course, you may substitute other foods to make up for the calorie loss—for example, part of your plan at cocktail parties may be to munch on the hors d'oeuvres instead of refilling your glass. But there's a good chance it will work the other way around, too. You're likely to want to eat less when you drink less. Moderate alcohol consumption can be an appetite stimulant, remember? There's a good chance you won't be tempted to gorge on handfuls of peanuts.

So don't just keep track of the calories you save. Weigh yourself. If you don't increase your eating at the same time, you should lose weight.

As for money savings, set aside $2 for every drink cut from your weekly consumption. Let the pot build for a few months. It's no get-rich-quick scheme, but that pile of fives and tens accumulated over four or five months is a nice pat on the back and padding in the pocket.

Step 5
The Month-by-Month Chart

You might want to approach your drink-reduction program in a businesslike manner. Set up a month-by-month chart, with one line showing your projected levels of social drinking and another showing your actual consumption. If you come up short of your projections, you either have to work harder or have to adjust the projections to more reasonable levels.

All of this paperwork may seem cumbersome, a little silly, and a good way to take all the fun out of drinking. But it's much less time-consuming process than balancing your checkbook. And it isn't as if you'll be going to parties with booklets full of charts and tables to lug around. Don't be overly serious about it. Just be conscientious and fair with yourself. When the numbers show up on paper, they're good reminders of your progress. Knowing that you are making progress is great, and actually seeing a record of that progress in front of you is that much more satisfying.

A *final note:* If you have a computer at home, there are certain software programs that will adapt well to this program. It will be easier to save information—daily records, for example—and compare days, weeks, and months.

Putting Your Plan into Action

So you've decided to take the step: You've developed a new frame of mind about drinking and you've devised a plan that will keep your drinking within a level you are comfortable with. You know that by cutting back on your drinking your life is going to be a lot more fun and productive.

Wonderful. It is all so well intentioned, but then you're going to go to the next cocktail party and rediscover how easy it is to slip back into your old drinking patterns. Oh, well—the idea was a good one anyway.

But that needn't happen! You obviously need more than a goal of keeping your drinking to certain levels. You're going to need tactics that will make your plan work and make it possible to achieve your goal.

That's where the next part of this book comes in. It is filled with tips that will help you put your plan into action and then stick with it. Many of the tips have been suggested and are used by some of the most influential and successful people in the worlds of business, entertainment, and the arts. These are people who socialize often—either by choice or professional necessity. Some regularly attend four or more social functions a day. They know that they can't afford to overindulge when they are in highly visible situations and their reputations are at stake.

How you decide to use the tips is up to you. You'll find that some are more effective for you than others. You'll also find that some are more effective in certain situations than in others. To some extent, how you use the tips will depend on the kind of drinker you are. For example, you may be the kind who finds it easy to stay sober at business functions but who really cuts loose when friends get together.

Each of the tips has been numbered to help you keep a personal record of those that work best for you. You might want to jot down the most effective tips in the front of the book, so you'll have them handy for quick reference. After a while, if you stick with your plan, the reference will become superfluous—the tips that work for you will become second nature.

COCKTAIL PARTIES

Tips for Cutting Down

Assuming that you are someone who enjoys drinking but who is also trying to keep from going overboard, attending a cocktail party is like walking through a minefield of temptation. The enticements to have another drink are powerful—after all, they don't call them "cocktail parties" for nothing.

After being greeted, the first question you are probably going to hear from the attentive host is, "Can I get you a drink?" It's hardly an open-ended question. The host is expecting you to accept the offer, and you'd better be ready with a pretty convincing comeback if you don't want one right away. If you hem and haw, the host will probably throw in some encouragement, and you'll end up having something.

How to Cut Down Your Social Drinking

It's easy to get caught in a bind at a cocktail party. Most cocktail parties go on for at least two hours. Even if you make an effort to sip your drink slowly, two hours is plenty of time to have three or four drinks—whether you're a sipper or a gulper. If you come early (hoping to sneak out early) you may find that the host is overattentive because you're among the first arrivals. Your drink may be refilled before you get a chance to refuse. Come late, and the hors d'oeuvres you planned to munch on instead of sipping a drink are gone. Also, the liquor usually flows more freely the later the party drags on. Timing is a crucial factor in keeping your drink consumption down, but despite your best efforts, it's easy to arrive a little earlier or a little later than you expected.

Even at larger cocktail receptions, where you may get a chance to mingle for a while before having a drink, there always seems to be a bar no matter which way you turn. At many formal receptions, waiters and waitresses wander around with trays full of glasses of wine and champagne. It's pretty unusual to find them offering something nonalcoholic such as orange juice or club soda.

Even without the band of waiters and waitresses, you'll encounter friends who will offer to get you a drink when *their* glasses are empty. It's funny how that works—people have a habit of offering a refill when they want one, not necessarily when you do.

In short, if you want to cut your consumption, your resistance has to be stronger at cocktail parties than at any other occasion. Your plan has to be better organized and your desire to stick with it has to be stronger.

When choosing tips—or devising tips of your own—remember that often the tips that work best are the simplest ones.

Cocktail Parties

You don't want to arrive at a cocktail party with some Rube Goldberg scheme so elaborate that either you can't remember all the steps or you draw attention to yourself.

Many successful people are able to keep their liquor consumption down by setting one or two firm rules about their drinking and sticking with them. You may need a little gimmick when you first try to stay within your drink limit, but in the long run, you'll do well by having a rule or two about your drinking that you absolutely won't break. For example:

Tip #1
Stop Early

Probably the biggest mistake that social drinkers make is not knowing when to stop. There may at some time have been a legitimate cocktail *hour,* but not anymore. When you go to a cocktail party, it lasts at least two hours, maybe even the whole evening.

Jake Leo, a successful yacht broker in Mamaroneck, New York, is obligated, both for business reasons and because of the circle of friends he travels in, to attend a lot of receptions and cocktail parties at yacht clubs in the New York and Connecticut area.

"The parties can go on for hours," Leo says. "There are too many 'good times' and too many people who want to have one more at the bar." Yachting (at least sailor talk of adventures on the high seas) and drinking seem to have a synergistic effect on each other, and thus yacht club parties have a habit of being *very* wet.

"I took stock of what I was doing and set a few rules," Leo continues. "Now, any time I can actually feel the liquor, I stop. Period. I don't want anything running me."

Like Leo, you don't have to drink right up until the last call. Stop when you know you've had as much as you can reasonably handle. Of course, you may not always be a good judge of that. So better yet, set an absolute cut-off time before you go to the party, and drink only nonalcoholic beverages after that.

Best of all, schedule another event—a play, a movie, a dinner—so you'll have to leave at a certain time. Lingering at a cocktail party is asking for trouble.

Tip #2
Start Late

The opposite tactic works just as well—perhaps better. Come to the party late, and don't start drinking the minute you get there. You might want to establish a new routine for yourself by setting a time of day before which you will absolutely not have a drink. That's the way Richard Almeida, Citibank vice-president in Los Angeles, keeps from going overboard.

"I have several methods of keeping my overall alcohol consumption at a reasonable level—and my weight down," says Almeida. "If I've been to too many social occasions within a given period—a day, an evening, a week—I switch to Perrier water and lime.

"If I don't know the people I'm meeting, I can pull the old trick of saying that I'm on medication and have to stay away from alcohol.

"But the best rule I stick to is not to have a cocktail until after 7:00 P.M. Anything before that means that I'll have just too many drinks before the end of the evening."

That kind of limit is easy to remember and can become second nature very easily. It can become like your subconscious time clock that tells when it's time to eat. How often would you—or anyone you know—consider having lunch before noon?

Tip #3
Start in Neutral

Don't have a drink before heading off to a party or reception. That's a trap couples can fall into. While the woman is putting on last-minute makeup, the man mixes himself a drink. Silly, really silly.

If you can't stand waiting once you're ready to go, start dressing for the party later. Make a firm agreement with your spouse that you'll both be ready at the same time. Whatever you do, start in neutral. You'll have plenty of chances to drink once you get to the party.

Tip #4
Sex First

If you're not going to have a drink before going to a party, you might consider this alternative use of the time. It comes from a prominent Dallas physician who is a leading authority on alcohol and health. He reports that a number of his patients who are trying to cut down on their drinking find that having sex beforehand makes them less likely to drink too much at a party. Sex, he says, helps ease the tensions that might otherwise impel you toward the bar.

(A serendipitous benefit of this technique might be that, thus engaged, you'd probably be late for cocktail hour.)

Tip #5
Candy Is Dandy

Another physician, who serves on the President's Council on Alcohol Abuse, suggests a different kind of pre-party treat that has the same effect: Have a couple of chocolates just before you leave home. Like sex, chocolate is an appetite quencher and—as anyone who has ever gained weight after stopping smoking knows—one appetite can be made to substitute for another. Chocolate, the doctor adds, is slightly greasy and therefore lines your stomach a bit, insulating it from the alcohol.

So if real kisses aren't available, try chocolate ones.

Tip #6
Switch On and Off

Remember, at least half of the relaxing effect of having a drink at a cocktail party is simply having something to do with your hands. Too often you'll find yourself getting a second, third, and fourth drink just so you'll have something to sip from.

Don Miles, an architect and urban planner in Seattle, has devised a simple way to get around that problem. "I drink an eight-ounce glass of water before each drink at a party," Miles says. "That means that every drink is diluted by the time it gets into my system. The water also fills me up, so I don't feel as much like drinking alcohol.

"This allows me to have a drink in my hand during the entire party. I also keep away from all those calories that you get in a drink."

In taking Miles's advice, it's also a good idea to *finish* with a glass of water instead of a drink. The more water you take in, the easier it is for your system to metabolize the alcohol. You'll also be less tempted to have a "drink for the road," since you know you'll have to pour down another glass of water if you do.

Tip #7
Just Add Water

A variation on Tip #6 is to add water to your drink as you go along. Again, you get the socializing benefit of having a drink in your hand without consuming all that alcohol. You also avoid having to switch glasses every time you get another drink.

Sidney Offit of Bridgehampton, N.Y., is a wearer of many hats—a novelist, teacher, editor, television commentator, and writer of children's books. That multifaceted business life can mean a multi-event social calendar. And often, the parties drag on. "The only way to get through some of those long cocktail parties is to water down my drink," says Offit. "Every time the glass is half empty, I simply add water to the drink instead of liquor.

"I even add water to the wine if it's a long dinner party and the host isn't looking."

Tip #8
Stagger and Stay Sober

A second variation on Tip #6 is used by the president of a prestigious country club in Atlanta. Using her terminology, she "staggers" her drinks in order to keep her liquor consumption down.

Here's how it works.

The first drink is a full glass of wine, sipped slowly and enjoyed fully. The second drink is half wine, half soda—the classic spritzer. After that, add soda whenever the glass is half empty.

It's kind of like the old axiom about walking halfway to a wall. If you keep halving the distance, you never reach the wall, of course. If you keep diluting your drink, you'll never reach the point of no return.

Also, if you are a "staggerer" who enjoys wine, you can still have a glass of wine with dinner and enjoy its taste without danger of overdrinking.

Tip #9
All You Ever Wanted in a Drink

Of course sometimes the best thing to do is keep it simple—don't drink at all, even if the occasion is called a "cocktail party." That doesn't mean you have to have something alcoholic. And it doesn't mean you have to stick to water either. There are plenty of tasty nonalcoholic drinks available at the well-stocked bar. Seymour Durst, a successful Manhattan real estate developer, faces a busy schedule of receptions, dinners, and lectures, and he'd probably be something of a vegetable if he had an alcoholic drink at every social occasion.

So instead of turning into a vegetable, Durst turns to vegetable juice. When asked how he keeps his alcoholic consumption down, Durst replies: "V-8."

Tip #10
Someone's Watching You

A good way to keep yourself from having too much is to remind yourself constantly of your professional stature. You may forget it momentarily at a party, but others don't. Maintain a professional decorum. Even at social functions that are primarily social, someone is likely to be watching you and making judgments about your professional character.

"As a professional, I am very careful about what—and how much—I drink in public," says Carolyn Farb, a professional fund raiser and journalist in River Oaks, Texas.

"I get quite upset when I see other professionals such as doctors and lawyers drinking too much at any function. I certainly wouldn't want to see a doctor having 'too good a time' when I know he or she is going to have to operate in the morning."

You don't have to be crawling on the floor to tarnish your professional image. A slurred word or a memory lapse can be enough to cast doubts. There's no reason to jeopardize your professional reputation for a couple of ounces of liquor.

Tip #11
Duck the Waiter

At especially elegant receptions, don't be lured by the convenience of having waiters to take orders and serve drinks. Think of those waiters as being an extra touch of elegance warranted by that particular occasion, like white linen and silver serving dishes. Don't think of them as being the people who will get you a drink whenever you want one.

As executive vice-president of Ticor Mortgage Company in Los Angeles, John Hooff is obligated to attend a number of formal receptions. His method of avoiding the extra drink: "I find that if I stay away from the service person who is taking drink orders or passing out champagne I can keep my overall consumption down at a reception.

"Of course, a waiter may catch up with you if you are in a

conversation with someone. But that doesn't mean I have to accept when he offers a drink."

A good rule to follow at a formal reception is: Always decline drinks offered by a service person.

If you want a drink, go to the bar and order it yourself. That will discourage you from too many drinks for many reasons. First, you have to make an extra effort. Second, you may not want to wend your way through a crowded room to get to the bar. Third, you wouldn't want to break away from a conversation to order a drink. And fourth, you'll look like a real lush if you make regular trips to the bar.

Tip #12
Better Them Than Me

This tip might seem a bit diabolical, but you might have to resort to it when you get stuck with a hard-drinking crowd that insists you join in the festivities.

It comes from Jerry Reinsdorf, chairman and a principal owner of the Chicago White Sox baseball team. Reinsdorf recalls the incident in which he first pulled off his little trick successfully: "We were at a cocktail party for a lot of team owners, and they were serving something called Tennessee tea. The stuff was a concoction of five or six different liquors. I knew I'd get loaded if I had very much, and I still had important business to take care of.

"So I decided to pour most of my drink into the glass of Eddie Einhorn [the White Sox president] when he went to the men's room. The trick worked so well that I did the same thing whenever someone left the room. I stayed pretty sober that night in comparison to the others."

Cruel and unusual punishment? Perhaps. You certainly wouldn't want to pull that sort of gimmick on people who have to drive home later.

If you're at a cocktail party or reception, and particularly if you're there to do business, discreetly pour off some of your drink when the host isn't looking. Choose a sensible receptacle—and take it easy on friends and flora.

Reinsdorf isn't the only person named Jerry who takes the jocular approach to the subject of cocktail party survival. Jerry Della Femina, well-known advertising man and author of *From Those Wonderful Folks Who Gave You Pearl Harbor*, would have us believe he's a guzzler. "I drink anything that's put in front of me," he says with a straight face. "I just make certain that I'm at a crowded cocktail party so that I can't fall down." (Sure, Jerry. How come nobody's ever seen you have more than two?)

Tip #13
A Little Reverse Psychology

If you decide to order something nonalcoholic as an alternative to the drink you enjoy, you might get antsy thinking about the drink you're missing. Later, when you *do* have a drink, you may end up gulping it down as a long-awaited reward.

Instead of falling into that trap, William Rice, editor-in-chief

Cocktail Parties

of *Food and Wine* magazine, goes to the opposite extreme. He orders the most alcoholic drink he can think of. "I usually hold off for a while at a cocktail party and then use a little reverse psychology on myself," Rice says. "I order a martini and sip it slowly, fully aware that I've got a pretty powerful drink in my hand. I know that it won't be long before it gets warm, and a warm martini is pretty tasteless and dead."

Making your drink unappealing may seem like an odd tactic. But it works. The longer a drink stays in your hand, the less appetizing it becomes. You probably wouldn't want a flat gin and tonic or a diluted Bloody Mary any more than you would a warm martini.

A Note About Drinking at Office Parties

Parties at the office are usually held for a specific purpose—to celebrate a holiday, to celebrate the successful implementation of a business plan, to introduce a new partner, to reward people for a job well done, etc. Regardless of the purpose of the party, it always provides a good opportunity for you to get to know your co-workers in a more relaxed atmosphere. Take advantage of the opportunity. But watch out.

Most office parties range somewhere between being business/social occasions and being flat-out business functions (see second chapter, "Typical Social Drinkers"). The liquor may be flowing freely and your boss may be encouraging you to have another drink, but be judicious. You are being watched, however casually, both by the people who work for you and the people you work for. After all, you're probably doing the same thing.

Keep in mind: People respect you for your work habits, but they remember you longer for your social habits. You might be an absolute crackerjack at your job, and you might be the most reliable person in the office. But if you have too much to drink at an office party, the reputation that will stick with you longest is that you are a horse's ass at a party.

Thus, you can't afford even the slightest overindulgence while at the office. Fortunately, most office parties have a built-in escape clause: Your spouse is expecting you home, or you have to be somewhere at a certain time. Don't feel obligated to stay just because your boss or your colleagues are still at the party.

If you are really having a good time (and often, office parties can produce truly rewarding revelations about how nice the people are that you work with), suggest discreetly to a few close associates that you'd like to continue the party elsewhere—a nearby restaurant or someone's home. If so, make sure not to offend people who feel that they should be included.

Office parties can be fun and rewarding, but don't be fooled—they are definitely all business.

DINNERS AND LUNCHES

The Inevitable Pressures and Temptations

Europeans often regard Americans as being a little peculiar about their dining-out habits. For many Europeans, dining out is an evening's event that would be cut short if it lasted less than two hours. Americans, on the other hand, tend to squeeze dinner in before a show, after a cocktail party, or as a supplement to some other activity. Dining out is not the main event.

There is nothing wrong with that, of course. However, it can lead to some bad habits. Typically, you may be seated at a restaurant and order a round of drinks as quickly as possible—probably before seeing a menu. That means there's a good chance you'll order a second drink before the meal arrives. By the time you are drinking wine with your dinner, your taste buds are sufficiently dulled so that you won't be able to tell whether you're really getting haute cuisine or fast food.

Dining out with your family, friends, or a special friend should be a festive occasion. The highlights are the company you are with and the food. But by drinking too much too fast, you can take some of the interest out of both. You don't have to spend three hours in a restaurant savoring five courses, but you shouldn't gulp down two or three quick drinks before your dinner arrives, either.

That's easily said, but the pressures and temptations to drink while dining out can be powerful and cleverly disguised. Restaurants make most of their money from the take at the bar. Restaurants want you to drink more. So does the busy waiter or waitress, for whom serving drinks is much less involved than serving food.

Most restaurants go to great lengths to create environments that lend themselves to a relaxed or romantic mood. All that soft lighting and comfortable seating makes for subtle encouragement for you to have another.

When you're dining at a friend's house, you'll face a different set of pressures and temptations. In contrast to the quick-in, quick-out style you tend to encounter when dining at a restaurant, dining at a friend's house is probably the evening's entertainment. You may find yourself getting trapped in a variety of drinking situations before dinner, during dinner, and after dinner. Even when you're trying to take it easy, you may find yourself consuming three or more drinks because of a sense of obligation you feel toward the host. Of course you can say what-

Dinners and Lunches

ever you want in turning down a drink, but in doing so, you may feel as if you are being impolite.

Many of the tips that work at cocktail parties also work for dinner parties at a friend's house. However, there are temptations to drink that are unique at dinner parties. For example, it is hard to resist when the host pulls out a couple of bottles of Chateau Lafite-Rothschild 1952 to serve with dinner. What you have to keep in mind above all, just as when dining at a restaurant, is that the food and the company are the high-lights of the show, and you don't want to spoil them.

A business lunch or dinner is a different ballgame. You may be less tempted to drink at lunch when you know you have an afternoon full of business responsibilities. But when you sit down to have lunch with a business associate or client who wants to have a drink and expects you to have one, too—well, it puts you in a tough bind. At the same time, that busy waiter is offering you a drink for the second or third time.

"You don't have to resort to a brusque "No" when the host or waiter offers you a drink. There are clever ways of avoiding an extra drink when dining out, so you can be sure you'll savor the food and appreciate the company. Besides, with that delicious meal to look forward to, you hardly need the extra calories that you're going to get from drinking.

Tips for Cutting Down

The tips in this chapter are for three different (though obviously related) situations:

- Business lunches
- Dinners at restaurants
- Dinners at the homes of friends

In many cases, you will find that they are interchangeable, just as those tips you might use at cocktail parties can work just as well when you're dining out. Again, it is up to you to decide when, where, and how to put these tips to best use for *you*.

Tip #14
Dine with Fine Wine

There are basically two kinds of wine—fine wine and table wine. Most people order table wine when they dine out. There is a tendency to regard wine as just another alcoholic beverage—indeed, the proper drink when you are dining.

Yet according to Jerry Berns of New York's prestigious "21" Club, diners cheat themselves out of a real taste treat when they drink large amounts of table wine. Instead, says Berns, "we feel that a proper bottle of wine should be ordered with the meal and that it should be savored and enjoyed." In other words, order one bottle of fine wine instead of two bottles of more ordinary table wine. And in order for that bottle of wine to be "savored and enjoyed," you shouldn't dull your taste buds by having two or three drinks beforehand. Save your money, and spend it on a bottle of wine that is truly elegant.

But how do you tell which bottle of wine is "proper"? "Proper," says Berns, "reflects the quality of the person you are with and the ultimate purpose of the encounter."

Tip #15
Order Wine First

If you really enjoy having a drink before dinner, there's no reason you can't adapt Berns's advice, as does Lili Fable, the president of New York's Ninth Avenue Association. "We have eliminated the cocktails before dinner by ordering a fine bottle of wine first," says Fable. "That way, we cut out the extra alcohol we don't need, and we can enjoy the wine more fully."

Fable arrived at this strategy in stages. "We also tried ordering wine by the glass first," she says. "But that seemed silly. The first glass of wine should be the best. That's when your sense of taste and smell are sharpest. Anyway, you never write home or tell your friends about house wines. Now we order a good bottle of wine right away and enjoy it through the meal."

Order fine wine, order it right away, and savor it as one of the great pleasures of dining out.

Tip #16
Half Empty Is Better Than Empty

When dining out, you may feel you have to finish everything you paid for. It is a common habit to gulp down the remains of a drink and hand the empty glass to the waiter before launching into the meal.

Fredric Axelrod, vice-president at the Berenter Greenhouse & Webster advertising agency in Manhattan, has come upon a sensible way of avoiding that trap. "I believe in being realistic when ordering drinks," says Axelrod. "My wife doesn't drink, and therefore a full bottle of wine with dinner is too much to order. I used to order a full bottle of wine, and then I felt obligated to drink it all. But I've consciously changed my attitude on this. After all, I bought it. I can do what I want with it. I don't always eat all that's on my plate, so why should I feel I have to finish every drink?

"Now I'm not afraid to leave a half-filled drink at a cocktail party or dinner party. It doesn't bother me if I leave a partially consumed bottle of wine if we are out with another couple. No one says that you have to drink all the liquor in your glass."

Tip #17
Food First, Liquor Later

What's the first thing you do when you sit down in a restaurant for dinner? If you order a drink, you're not alone. That, of course, is the way things are usually done. And you're not alone if you then sit for a while talking, occasionally glancing at the menu, while the waiter does his rounds. It may be twenty minutes or more before you actually get around to ordering food.

And then you wait, because good food takes time to prepare. Even cold dishes have to be properly arranged and seasoned. It's a rare occasion when your food comes *sooner* than you want.

So instead of ordering your drink first, order food first. Ask right away for the menu and the day's specials, and ask the waiter to return in a couple of minutes. Once you've placed your order, you can then ask for a drink. By doing that, you'll have just about the right amount of time for one drink before your food is served.

This is a good tactic to use at a business lunch, as well as at dinner. Once you get involved in a business discussion, having to stop to order your food can be an intrusion. So suggest to your lunch partner that you order your lunch first and then a drink—all before you get down to discussing business. That way, you'll drink less and have fewer intrusions from the waiter.

Tip #18
Let Your Schedule Do the Talking

Chuck Scarborough, the news anchorman for NBC-TV in New York, is fortunate enough to have a built-in excuse for turning down drinks at dinner parties. "I have to do the 11:00 P.M. news, and therefore I'm probably the worst dinner guest in the city," says Scarborough. "There is just no way I can have a couple of glasses of wine with dinner and then write the news of the day.

"My friends now understand that I can't have a drink at dinner. They know they should offer me a glass of soda water when I arrive instead."

Of course, not everyone has a work schedule like Scarborough's. But having work pending is a legitimate and accepted excuse when turning down a drink. It isn't unreasonable to think that you may have unfinished work you brought home, or that you may want to start early and fresh the next morning. And if you say so, don't be surprised when people are impressed by your sense of professionalism. Keep in mind: Drinking does little for your productivity, whether it be work you have to do that night, like Scarborough, or work you have to do the next day.

Tip #19
Work First

Another way of keeping your drinking to a minimum while making sure you get your work done is to finish as much work as you can before leaving the office. There is nothing that says you can't stay an extra hour to take care of unfinished business. In fact, if you work a nine-to-five job, early evening can be a quiet and productive time.

Mary Nichols, director of radio and television at WNYC in New York, follows a simple rule: Work first, dine late. "I often have to work late into the evening," says Nichols. "I can't do that if I have a couple of drinks with dinner.

"I now schedule my dinners as late as possible so that I can get all of my work done and relax during the meal."

If you're going to a friend's house, you'd rather not arrive late for dinner. But by following Nichols's advice, you can avoid getting stuck in an extended pre-dinner "cocktail hour" by putting those early evenings to more constructive use. Also, when dinner rolls around and food, not drink, is the featured attraction, you'll really be ready to dig in.

How to Cut Down Your Social Drinking

Tip #20
Wait for the Wine

Good hosts like to serve good wine with dinner. But if you have two or three drinks before dinner, you'll not only deprive yourself of the fine-wine experience, you'll also be doing a slight injustice to the host who spent money, thought, and effort in getting the right wine.

Gael Greene, the food critic for *New York* magazine, appreciates a good glass of wine enough to be willing to take her chances on the dinner wine. "I find that it's too easy to drink without thinking during cocktails," says Greene. "And the wine that's served then is usually not worth drinking anyway. So I wait, full of hope, for a great red wine at dinner.

"To calm the anxious hostess, I walk around with a glass of New York's delicious tap water on the rocks—with a dash of lemon or lime.

"But my overall rule is this: I don't drink standing up."

Tip #21
Swoon to the Aroma

Gael Greene has another method of avoiding too much to drink, and she puts it into action when drinks are offered after dinner. She'll accept the offer, but not for the liquor. She likes the fragrance. "I sniff poire or framboise after dinner," she says.

Dinners and Lunches

"But I never drink it. That's easy for me, because I love the intense perfume and loathe the fierce taste."

You can take Greene's trick a step further. The next few times you order drinks, take note of their sensuous nature. When you have a good meal, you probably appreciate the aroma, the flavor, and the way it's presented at the table. Do the same with your drink. Admittedly, a drink such as vodka on the rocks ranks pretty low in sensuousness, so be imaginative and order something a little more elegant than usual.

Tip #22
Let the Sun Shine In

Those clever restaurateurs. They have a habit of dressing their establishments up with dark, romantic lighting and all the ambience you'd ever want—just to encourage you to order another drink. As noted, they make most of their money from bar sales, so they like it when you have two or three drinks, even though you've set your limit at just one.

Simple psychology: Darkly lit places encourage drinking, whereas light, airy places discourage it. Think of the difference between going to one of those old, wood-paneled men's clubs for lunch and going to an outdoor bistro.

If you're with someone you love, you'll probably prefer the romantically lit place. But if you want to do business over lunch, stick to brightly lit restaurants that put the emphasis on food, not drink. If you have papers to exchange, you'll have the added benefit of being able to see them where the lighting is good.

Tip #23
Keep It Light, Make It Festive

Despite your best efforts, there may be business encounters in which having a drink is unavoidable. In some cases, you may just feel like having something a little stronger than soda water.

If so, be sensible about it. You don't have to order a drink that's going to knock your socks off and affect your ability to do business. You definitely don't have to order something that's as strong as the drink your lunch partner is having.

"I restrict my drinking diet to a light beer," says Robert F. Bedell, who runs his own Washington, D.C., consulting firm. "I don't see how anyone can conduct business after having a martini. I certainly couldn't conduct a management seminar if I had a hard drink for lunch."

Boring? "It all depends on how you approach it," says Bedell. "If I'm going to be in a festive mood, I ask that my beer be served in a champagne glass."

Tip #24
Arrive Early

There are lunch partners who can be pretty insistent about your joining them for a drink. If you know that before the lunch appointment, you can avoid an awkward situation by beating your lunch partner to the draw.

Dinners and Lunches

Adrienne Cleere, a vice-president for American Express in Los Angeles, often conducts business over lunch. "I think that most people would rather you have a drink with them if they want one, so they don't feel uncomfortable drinking alone," Cleere says, "so I make a point of arriving at the restaurant five minutes early. I order a Virgin Mary and have it at the table when my lunch partner arrives. He or she can order anything, and I'm not in a position of being intimidating to my lunch partner because I'm not having a drink.

"If he or she wants a second drink, fine. I just ask the waiter for 'another round of the same.'"

If you conduct business regularly over lunch, and if you have a restaurant you regularly go to, it's not a bad idea to let the bartender or headwaiter know that you have a standard non-alcoholic drink—a Virgin Mary or a tonic water with lime. That way, you can feel perfectly comfortable ordering "the usual," and your lunch partner will never know the difference.

Tip #25
Set the Tone

"If you want to avoid a boozy meal," says Jerry Orbach, star of the hit musical *42nd Street*, "take the initiative when the waiter comes to the table. Be the first to order. The first drink sets the tone. If you order a Perrier or a wine spritzer, nobody's going to order a martini."

Tip #26
A Secret Arrangement

Robert Merrill, the Metropolitan Opera's great baritone, tells of a technique he developed to deal with a special situation: lunching with bibulous restaurateur Toots Shor. It was part of Toots's routine to make his favorite guests have a drink, or two or three, with him.

To cope with this constant pressure from Toots, Merrill had a private discussion with the bartender. "We came up with a special drink for me, a combination of orange juice, soda, and lime. It looked exactly like a screwdriver. The bartender always served up 'my drink' the minute I entered the restaurant, and Toots was none the wiser."

Many of us lunch at the same restaurant frequently and know the bartender or a certain waiter. Like Robert Merrill, you too can make a secret arrangement that will jump right over the whole discussion of whether or not you're drinking.

Tip #27
Breakfast Instead

The business "lunch" has become the most accepted way of working and eating at the same time. Yet there is no written rule that says lunchtime is the only time of day you have to get together for business.

Dinners and Lunches

Breakfast is the most overlooked meeting time. It doesn't cut into the middle of your workday, and it is the one meal where you never have to feel obligated to have a drink.

New York's power brokers regularly jockey for good tables at the prestigious Regency Hotel to discuss business. In most cases, a restaurant that serves breakfast and lunch will be less crowded and more quiet at breakfast. You'll be able to accomplish much more and obviously drink much less.

Suggesting breakfast instead is a particularly good tactic if you're expecting to get together with someone who likes to have a drink.

Tip #28
Feel Secure

You may find, once you get into it, that you feel secure about having something nonalcoholic at a business lunch, that you don't want to be devious and *look* as if you're having something alcoholic. More power to you! Drink whatever you want and be open about it.

That advice comes from Letitia Baldrige, an author who should know—she has written a book on manners. When she meets someone for a business lunch, Baldrige orders a diet soft drink and doesn't dress it up with a lime or a lemon twist. "Feeling free to order what you want is a sign of security," says Baldrige. "People who you do business with will respect you for that."

Tony Randall, whose celebrity as an actor keeps him moving from one potential drinking occasion to the next, adopts the same no-nonsense, no-apology approach. "My life is full of activity, and I don't want to miss a single minute of it," says Randall. "So when I go somewhere, I just ask for a Perrier and nurse it for a long time."

A Note About Doing Business and Staying Sober

Take a typical business lunch situation you are likely to encounter: You're scheduled to meet an important business associate for lunch, perhaps a client or potential client, your boss, or someone with whom you're trying to strike up a deal—in short, someone with whom good business relations are essential.

This is a person who you know likes to have a drink or two (maybe three) with lunch and who, by friendly nature, will insist that you join in. The pressure is on. The concept of "conflict of interest" sounds vaguely in the back of your brain. You don't want your lunch partner to feel uncomfortable by having to drink alone, and yet you want to be clearheaded in order to conduct business. You don't want to lose the opportunity for a promotion or a lucrative deal because you weren't able to do business in a productive, professional manner.

For some reason, having drinks with lunch has managed to carve itself a niche as an integral part of the way America does business. Not all deals are consummated in restaurants and cocktail lounges, of course, but sooner or later (and probably

Dinners and Lunches

sooner) the successful business person will encounter the situation.

You can put any of the tips suggested in this chapter to work, if possible, but sometimes there's just no way out of having a drink you really don't want to have.

The way to handle it: Think of drinking and doing business as being on opposite sides of a scale. The less important the business being discussed over lunch, the less important it is to maintain a polite profile when you're offered a drink. If you're meeting with the president of IBM and he invites you to have a drink, it probably makes sense to take him up on it. If you're meeting with your banker to discuss restructuring your mortgage, there's no reason you should feel you have to accept when he offers to buy you a drink.

Also, carefully consider your ability to conduct business after having a drink or two. You should have a very precise idea of how much you can drink and still function with a clear head. Just because your lunch partner can have a couple of drinks and still conduct business, that doesn't mean you can. Remind yourself beforehand of how much you can drink, and don't exceed that level. Remember, you're there to do business, so if you have any doubts, drink less than you think you can handle.

A rule of thumb: Have at least one drink less than your lunch partner. A person may insist that you have a drink; however, you should feel that your obligation ends after the first drink. There's nothing wrong with sipping the first drink slowly (though letting it sit there untouched can be more impolite than ordering nothing). Never feel that you have to have a second drink because your lunch partner is having another.

The bottom line is: You're there to do business, and you do

business better when you're sober. It's a lot easier to blow a big deal by having too much rather than too little.

Ed Asner says, in the bulletin published by the Will Rogers Institute, White Plains, New York, "Alcohol burns, in more ways than one. Excessive drinking burns American business to the tune of 54 billion dollars a year."

ENTERTAINING AT HOME

What's Your Responsibility?

If you're planning to have a dinner party or a cocktail party at home, do your friends a favor while doing a favor for yourself. Keep the flow of liquor under control. You may feel reluctant to discourage a tipsy friend from having another, but if you handle your party just right, you can easily avoid situations like this.

There's no reason to feel that you have to get all your guests pie-eyed in order to earn yourself a reputation as a good host, even though people do have a tendency to remember a party fondly when it has been the kind of party they have trouble remembering at all. But your guests can have a good time at your party without consuming copious amounts of liquor. And

How to Cut Down Your Social Drinking

you don't have to hide the liquor bottles or serve only water and Hawaiian Punch in order to pull it off.

Think of a host as someone like the director of a play or movie. You are in control of what happens. You decide what the dinner menu will be and what time dinner will be served. You decide what kinds of activities people will be involved in. You decide when it is time for people to go home. And you also decide how much liquor will be served to your guests.

For starters, you as the host (or someone else that you designate) will be the bartender. Period. You're asking for trouble when you suggest that your friends mix drinks for themselves—because you're busy with dinner preparations or because you're locked in a conversation you don't want to leave. If you expect that the bartender duties will be too much for you to handle, hire someone to do the job for you. You should be able to hire a bartender for about $50, and it will be money well spent. You'll have more time to take care of other things and mingle with your friends. Also, a professional bartender adds a touch of elegance to a party. If you're concerned about the expense, you'll make some of it back by saving on the amount of liquor you serve.

If you hire someone, though, be precise in your instructions about mixing drinks. You don't want a bartender with a floppy wrist. And if possible, you should still make it your responsibility to check with your guests about refills. Again, you're the director. You decide when it's time for another round of drinks.

Oh, yes—you're the stage director, too. So don't set up the bar close to the center of activity if you can avoid it. Keep the bar in the kitchen pantry, or some other area that's out of view. After all, what do you think is going to happen when the bar is easily accessible to all guests? Not only is it easier for someone to refill his or her own drink, but it is also a powerful suggestion.

Entertaining at Home

You can anticipate times during any party when there will be lulls. Those lulls usually happen early on, as guests are arriving, and after dinner, when guests are slowed down by the great meal you've prepared. Have some kind of activity or plan to fill those lulls. Show photos from a recent trip. Ask advice or get your guests involved in a new project or hobby you've taken up. Play a game. You can even be a little sneaky and have your guests help with some of the chores by making them fun instead of tedious. Use your imagination, but make sure you give people plenty of opportunity to do something *other* than drink.

Finally, keep in mind that many of your friends will probably be driving home. Despite your efforts, someone may still have a little more than he or she can safely handle. Don't let your guests hit the road with happy, drunken grins on their faces. Offer alternatives to the guest who has been a little too eager to take you up on refill offers—a sofa or bed to sleep on for the night, a call for a cab ride home, or just the opportunity to stay a little longer to let the liquor wear off somewhat. A pitcher full of coffee may help, too, but it isn't an antidote to alcohol. Imagine a drunk driver who also has the jitters.

So be a good judge of which guest may have had more than enough. In fact, as the host, in some localities you may have a legal responsibility about what happens to your guests on the way home. Thus, you will not only be doing your guests a favor, but perhaps yourself as well.

When your guests are having a good time, they won't miss the extra drink. On the next few pages are some tips for how you can keep the flow of liquor down and still keep the fun in the party.

Tips for Cutting Down

Tip #29
No Control, No Return

Phyllis Cerf Wagner, senior vice-president at Wells Rich Greene advertising agency, is among New York's leading social organizers. She knows the dynamics of a good party, and she knows the pitfalls hosts shouldn't fall into when entertaining.

One is to make sure that your guests don't get more than just a little tipsy. The person who has had a little too much can cast a damper on the whole party. "If I had known," says Wagner, "that a guest was the type to overdo it, I wouldn't have invited him or her in the first place."

Of course you don't always know who's going to go overboard *before* you invite them. You can, however, make a point of not inviting them back the next time. It's a subtle but convincing way of getting the word out that you're not the kind of host who appreciates guests who like a little too much fun.

Entertaining at Home

Tip #30
If You Play,
You Stay

As the host, you should consider it part of your responsibility to keep track of how much your guests are drinking. It's up to you to try to keep things under control. Even so, there may be someone who's so insistent about having another drink that it's hard to say no.

So before you acquiesce, make a deal. James Colthup, a vice-president of John G. Dreisbach & Company in Santa Fe, is particularly concerned about drinking at high altitude, where drinks can be much more potent. "Therefore, we have a standing rule in our home," says Colthup. "If someone wants another drink and it is obvious that he or she has already had enough, we insist that they spend the night in the guest room. Then they can have all they want to drink—but they can't leave."

Of course, if you're too generous with your liquor, you may end up with a slumber party. You really shouldn't let your guests go over their limit at all.

Mrs. Cornelius Vanderbilt Whitney, the well-known artist of Saratoga Springs, New York, uses a similar technique. "At our New Year's Eve party," she says, "everyone is asked to stay overnight. That applies even to friends who live just a few miles away. It saves us from worrying when people go home."

Mrs. Whitney, as is clear from the above, cares about not drinking when driving. "When my husband and I go out to dinner," she says, "one of us won't drink that evening. We take turns being the one who isn't drinking. That way we're assured of getting home safely."

That technique would please Candy Lightner, the woman who, as founder of MADD—Mothers Against Drunk Driving— has had a major effect on the attitudes of Americans toward excessive drinking. She practices what she preaches. "My main concern is whether or not I am driving," she says. "If I am, then it's no more than one drink for me for the whole evening."

Tip #31
Precise Timing

A typical summer social scene: You invite friends over for barbecued chicken in your backyard. The guests arrive, and a little later you light the coals. You forgot, though, that it takes about forty-five minutes for the coals to really heat up. Oh, well— dinner is a little late, and everybody has another round (or two) of drinks.

That kind of fudging with time isn't a problem only among the barbecue crowd. How often have you planned dinner for eight-thirty and ended up serving some time after nine? Perhaps a few guests arrived late, you got caught in a conversation and forgot to turn on the oven, the wine wasn't chilled, or the cocktail hour just dragged on longer than expected.

There is nothing wrong with telling your guests when you invite them that dinner will be served *promptly* at eight or eight-thirty. It's impolite to come late to a dinner party, so don't feel bad about not waiting for the Joneses. And if you say eight-thirty, make sure the food is on the table at eight-thirty.

Not only can the extra half hour of cocktails before dinner mean another drink or two, but it also means that hungry guests will be filling up on hors d'oeuvres. They won't get a chance to really enjoy the meal you worked so hard to prepare.

Tip #32
Time Out, Dinner's Served

"When entertaining at home," says Sara Derr, president of St. James Travel in New York, "plan a first course or main course that requires precise timing in its preparation and announce it as you are taking your guests' coats at the door: 'So glad to see you, and I hope you're hungry? The soufflé (or Coquilles St. Jacques, or salmon puff or whatever) is due to come out of the oven in exactly 20 minutes.' This not only spares your guests a few drinks but assures that you don't get carried away at your own party."

Everyone has been to a cook-out where the host stands around the barbecued chicken, Scotch in hand, saying, "Oh hell, chicken is always good, we can eat anytime." Well, "anytime" becomes three hours, the chicken is dry and the guests are wet.

Tip #33
Where's the Waiter?

As a conscientious host, you like to make everything comfortable for your guests, but when it comes to serving drinks, you can make things *too* comfortable. People tend to accept refill offers almost unconsciously, particularly when they are caught in a conversation.

Mrs. George Martin (and her husband) of Rochester, New York, entertains frequently. She has found that providing too much convenience in refilling drinks can detract from the party.

"When entertaining at home, I never hire a waiter to take drink orders," says Mrs. Martin. "This tends to keep drinking down, because people don't want to excuse themselves from a good conversation and go to the bar to make themselves another drink. I've watched parties where there is a waiter, and almost everybody orders a drink when the waiter arrives."

It's not a bad idea, though, to have a bartender (or some other person you designate) manage your bar. People who are allowed to pour their own drinks tend to get heavy-handed as the evening progresses.

Tip #34
Avoid the Nightcap Trap

People usually don't leave the minute after dessert is served. Often they end up having another glass of wine, a snifter of cognac, or another mixed drink. If that's how you allow that time to be used, you're not doing your guests any favors—especially if they will be driving home soon.

Schedule some kind of activity for after dinner, preferably something in which everybody is involved. A game, a slide show, even just a walk outside to look at the stars—anything to stop people from resorting to another drink in order to keep themselves occupied. The activity doesn't have to take up the whole night, either. Once people have digested their food, they'll be less interested in having another drink.

Tip #35
The Right Desserts

Another way of avoiding the nightcap trap, says Susan DeDeyn of Atlanta, Georgia, is to serve desserts that discourage further drinking. "The general rule of thumb," she says, "is this: Desserts that are cold and chocolatey tend to discourage drinking; desserts with liquor in them tend to encourage drinking." Here's her brief list, to get you started:

Desserts that discourage drinking:
- Chocolate ice cream
- Sherbet
- Fresh fruit
- Most frozen deserts

Desserts that encourage drinking:
- Rum cake
- All flambéed dishes
- Cheese
- Danish pastries

Tip #36
Do It
the French Way

Still another way of avoiding falling into the nightcap trap is to follow the French example. After all, when it comes to dining, the French have a pretty well established reputation for knowing what they are doing.

"Instead of serving heavy liqueurs after dinner," says Daniel Coccoli, vice-president of the Novotel hotel chain headquartered in Paris, "we French often serve soft drinks or sparkling mineral water after dessert and coffee. That means there is a long time between the last glass of wine with dinner and the drive home."

To discourage even the thought of having another drink after dinner, put the liquor away when cocktail time is over. The sight of bottles of liquor after dinner may start some guests thinking about having one more. And it's a pretty pushy guest who asks for another drink once the liquor has been put away.

Tip #37
Make the Most
of Being a Host

When entertaining at home, it's more important to make sure your guests are having a good time than anything else. You can't be a good host, make sure the party is going smoothly, and drink too much at the same time.

Take it from Tony Michaels, the food and beverage manager at Miami's elegant Jockey Club. "The most important part of the job is to make sure the people you are with are comfortable," says Michaels. "I make it a habit not to have a drink with guests. Period. If I have a drink with one guest, I'll have to sit down for a drink with another. Pretty soon, that can lead to having too much. I have to make sure that the guests are taken care of."

Although Michaels is a "professional" host, his responsibility is no greater than yours when you are entertaining at home. You should make sure your guests are taken care of, and you can do that best when you drink less.

Tip #38
Drinking on the Job

Like Tony Michaels, many people work in places where drinks are served and so are faced with a special hazard. "I learned very early in my professional life," says Alphonse W. Salomone, senior vice-president of the Hilton Hotels Corporation, "that the hotel business can be hazardous in more ways than one. The nature of our business is public, and hotel executives lead rather public lives, and one can create a negative image very quickly by drinking unwisely. Few of us consume an inordinate amount, but the potential is always there, and we have to be conscious of it. After all, a hotel manager has a responsibility to every guest to be capable of making a sound decision—one that might affect lives—at all times of the day or night.

"My respect for the hotel business is pretty high, and speaking for myself, I want only to enhance its reputation. Our waiters and bartenders are aware that when I'm on the job, my drink is ginger ale."

Anyone who is in the hospitality industry would do well to consider Alphonse Salomone's advice. You can't take care of the public properly if you can't take care of yourself.

Tip #39
Give Guests Fair Warning

Here's another tip from high-altitude country—New Mexico—where people know they have to be really careful about their liquor consumption.

"We are seven thousand feet above sea level," says Margaret Gray, who runs her own company in Santa Fe. "Drinks can go right to your head. Our visitors from out of town may not be ready for that.

"So we recommend that they cut their alcohol consumption in half. And we serve water when guests arrive, during cocktails, and throughout dinner. The combination of these reminders tends to encourage people to monitor themselves."

You don't need the high-altitude excuse to remind your guests not to drink too much. You can be polite about it—warn them about drinking and driving home. Once the word is out, as Margaret Gray has discovered, people tend to watch out for themselves.

Tip #40
Feature the Juice, Not the Booze

Although you don't have to hide the liquor from your guests when entertaining at home, neither do you have to feature it at the bar with a dramatic flair.

Michael Battenberry, a food critic and author, sets up the bar in his home with large, elegant pitchers of fresh-squeezed orange juice, grapefruit juice, and other nonalcoholic delights. "And I try to light them up so they really look dazzling," says Battenberry. The bottles of liquor on the same table look decidedly less attractive.

Battenberry has been surprised to find how many of his guests opt for the fresh juice when it's presented in such an appealing fashion, and many stick with juice for the second drink instead of switching to liquor.

TIPS THAT WORK ANYTIME

By now you should have a pretty good idea of how to go about resisting the temptations of having more to drink than you want at various social occasions. Approach those situations with a sensible frame of mind, a good plan, and a commitment not to overdo it.

Yet you probably encounter many opportunities to drink that don't fit snugly into clearly defined categories. A friend calls and wants to get together for a drink after work. You enjoy having a quiet drink with your spouse when you get home after work. You like cracking open a nice cold beer after a tough tennis match (and a cold beer after long, hot exercise is one of the most pleasurable things in the world).

Although the likelihood of drinking too much in situations like these may not seem as great, the temptation is still there. You may have disciplined yourself well enough so that you won't

How to Cut Down Your Social Drinking

overdo it at a social function. Then you find yourself getting soused at the country club the next day, when the "drink" your foursome had after eighteen holes of golf turned into three or four. In the long run, you haven't really accomplished very much.

For most people who get pleasure from drinking, much of the drinking is done as a normal part of a daily or weekly routine. It's a pleasant way to fill up nonstructured time.

And that's where problems can easily arise. Most of us don't put much thought into how we use our spare time. After all, it *is* relaxing when you have no plans or obligations. But as you sit on your porch with drink in hand, as the evening gradually drifts to darkness, you've had three drinks without even thinking about it. You have a couple of open hours in the late afternoon, and after a friend suggests you get together for a beer, you find that the two of you have finished off a six-pack. If you like beer, it's easy enough to do.

Those extra drinks can be avoided, simply by being a little more constructive with your spare time. You don't have to have a great plan. Just think of something that's healthier, intellectually more stimulating, or just plain more fun than drinking. It shouldn't be hard to do.

It may mean changing your routine—like shuffling the deck and dealing yourself a new hand. The tips in this chapter will help prevent you from drinking more than you want anytime you're apt to encounter the opportunity to drink, whether it's at a party, the country club, or at home with your family. The tips will help you become more aware of those drinks that have a habit of slipping virtually unnoticed into your daily routine.

Tip #41
A Mile a Drink

As you cut down on your social drinking, you might just as well get in shape. Why not? A good way of doing that is by using exercise as a kind of punitive measure for overdoing it at the bar the night before.

Stuart Kessler, a senior partner at the accounting firm of Goldstein Golub Kessler in New York, reports that he runs three miles the next day for every drink the night before. "That keeps my drinking down to almost nothing," says Kessler, "and it keeps me in the best of shape."

You don't necessarily have to be as ambitious as the fitness-minded Mr. Kessler. After all, after four drinks he'll have to run a half marathon. But running one mile the next morning for each drink is a good start. If you already run regularly, just add a mile to your regular run for each drink the night before. Not only is running the next day a good way of keeping your liquor consumption down, it's also a good way of working out any lingering effects of the alcohol.

Be imaginative. Maybe you'd prefer to ride a bike five miles for each drink, or do fifty push-ups for each drink. Pick the exercise that's right for you. But make it tough on yourself. Five push-ups for every drink isn't going to do much for either your liquor consumption or your fitness.

Tip #42
Wreck Your Routine

If part of your daily routine is to walk in the door after work, hang up your hat, kiss the family, and mix a martini, plan something entirely different for tomorrow. Wreck your routine, and establish a new one.

Be imaginative. Come up with something that's fun and interesting. Tired after a day's work? Doing something physically active can actually be *more* relaxing than sitting around with a drink in your hand.

Friends and acquaintances have suggested a few possibilities:

- Jump in a pool (yours or someone else's).
- Walk your dog. If you don't have a dog, just walk.
- Run a mile.
- Play a game with your kids.
- Take a cold shower.
- Make love to your spouse.

Tip #43
Sign Up for Exercise

If you need a little push in order to wreck your routine, sign up for an activity that's scheduled for your usual cocktail time. With the so-called "fitness boom" in full swing, there are now plenty of opportunities to get involved in organized exercise programs—aerobics classes, running clubs, cycling clubs, etc. If you belong to a country club, or have access to good public facilities, you might want to sign up for tennis or golf lessons.

You may not be the sort who likes to exercise. In that case, sign up for a nonexercise class at your local college or community college. You can take courses in everything from gardening to playing the guitar.

After all, you're never too old to learn something new.

Tip #44
The 64-Ounce Diet

"A little water clears us of this deed," Lady Macbeth (a teetotaler) told her husband after they had done away with the king of Scotland. The ever-pragmatic Lady Macbeth.

To paraphrase, in a decidedly less gruesome context: A little water clears us of this need—the need for a drink, that is. Mrs. Wilson Eastland of Lexington, Kentucky, says, "I believe in a water diet that dictates that I drink sixty-four ounces of water per day. It really works.

"If I'm going to a party with my husband, I have a large glass of water before we leave for the party, and usually one when we get there. That fills me up."

It has been said before, but it is worth repeating: Water is a great substitute for a drink anytime. Part of the urge to drink comes from the body's need to replenish fluids. Simple mathematics: A ten-ounce glass of water provides more fluid than a six-ounce mixed drink. And alcohol actually causes dehydration. If you've just come off the tennis court or the golf course, have a glass of water or two before you order that beer. In fact, it's a good habit *always* to precede a drink with a glass of water.

Tip #45
School Nights Out

It's easy to fall into the pattern of having a drink or two every evening. The easiest way to break the pattern is: Just don't do it. Pick a couple of days during each week when your social calendar isn't filled and have nothing to drink at all.

If you want, of course, you can extend that rule: no mixed drinks on weekdays. Says Andrew Lyon Smith, senior vice-president of the United States Trust Company in Palm Beach, Florida: "I make it a practice not to have any hard drinks during the week. The hardest drink I'll have at a dinner party is a weak wine spritzer."

Smith also finds that it's best to deal with the pressure to drink as directly as possible. "If people push me to have an extra drink," Smith says, "I tell them that I don't drink during the week, and that I'm already over my limit."

Simple enough.

Tip #46
Make Your Drink a Ceremony

Enjoyment. That's the key word. A drink is something you should enjoy. It should be special. Having a drink should *never* be something you do because you have nothing better to do.

So, particularly if you are at home, make your drink a ceremony. Don't gulp down a glass of Scotch while you're loading the dishwasher. Very boring, and a waste of your fine Scotch. Also, those kinds of mindless drinks really make it hard to stick to your limit.

If you want a drink, take a shower, put on a comfortable bathrobe, and turn on some soft music. Sit back, close your eyes, and enjoy your drink.

"Make your drink special," says Clare Mannion, development manager of WTTW in Chicago. "If you like to drink to relax, relax first, then have your drink. If you expect to drink to take the edge off your hard day's work, you'll end up having two or three before you know it."

Tip #47
Only the Best

If you are going to employ the ceremonial approach, you might use the most ceremonial drink of them all. Says Bobby Short, renowned café pianist and singer: "I only drink champagne."

Tip #48
Start Right:
Quench Your Appetite

The urge to drink is spurred not only by your body's need to replenish fluids, but also by your body's need to replenish food. After all, the usual cocktail time is in the early evening, five or six hours after your last meal. Your mind may be telling you that you want a drink, whereas your body is trying to get across the message that you really need something to eat.

That's why it's easy to have two or three quick drinks in the evening, just as a way of filling yourself up. And it isn't a particularly satisfying fill-up, either—just a whole bunch of those empty alcoholic calories.

Priscilla Briggs, a nutrition counselor in Southport, Connecticut, makes a habit of eating a very light meal—about two hundred calories or so, before heading off for a social event. And when she arrives, she'll have a glass of water first. "I just tell the host that I'm very thirsty and that I'd like to start with a glass of

Tips That Work Anytime

water," says Briggs. "After I've finished the glass of water, and everyone else has finished their first drinks, I've noticed that no one really cares anymore what I'm drinking."

Not only has Briggs taken care of her need for food and fluid, she's also managed to defuse any social pressure she might feel to have a drink.

You can easily adapt Briggs's method to your routine. If you're the type of person who usually has a drink in the evening before having anything else, try something new. Eat a light snack—a salad, some fresh fruit, a couple of pieces of toast (use your imagination)—and wash it down with a big glass of water. You'll be consuming about the same number of or fewer calories than you would with a drink. Give yourself about a half hour to digest the food.

After you've done that, mix yourself a drink. The chances are you'll be much less tempted to have a second or third drink. You may not have made a significant slice into your calorie consumption, but you will have fueled your body with much more nutritious food.

Tip #49
Watch Out for the Bubbles

One of the quickest ways to get high from liquor (short of drinking straight out of the bottle) is to order drinks mixed with carbonated beverages. Not only does the effervescence give you a heady feeling, but it also tends to mask the flavor of the liquor.

If you're thirsty, it's easy to wash down a gin and tonic as if it were a ginger ale.

So stay away from those carbonated drinks, especially if you're really thirsty.

Tip #50
Bet Your Booze Off

Although in the long run you'll be more successful in keeping your liquor consumption down by reducing your drinking gradually, starting off with a bang isn't always a bad idea.

That suggestion comes from Dr. Duncan Finlay of Sarasota, Florida. When Dr. Finlay gets about fifteen pounds over his desired weight, he likes a little competition to spur his weight reduction. He bets a friend $100 that he can lose fifteen pounds in a month.

The easiest way to lose the weight? "Cut out the liquor and the beer," says Finlay. Although he reduces his eating habits somewhat, too, the biggest and easiest step is to stop drinking altogether for the month.

Again, this is a good way to start your drink-reduction program. When your nondrinking month is up, don't fall right back into your old drinking habits. Start a new routine that will feature drinking in moderation.

Tip #51
Punish Yourself

If you have trouble limiting yourself to just one or two drinks at any social function, try the tactic of being a little cruel to yourself. Making drinking a little less pleasurable and a little more agonizing.

That's the advice of L. Rust Hills, the fiction editor for *Esquire* magazine, who lives in Sarasota, Florida, and Stonington, Connecticut.

"It's helpful to choose drinks that taste somewhat medicinal," says Hills, "drinks like negronis and Campari and sodas. You'd have a hard time drinking too many of them—they taste too much like cough syrup. Also, the taste punishes you a little, which reminds you that you're doing something that, if not wrong, is at least in some respects serious."

Tip #52
Young Persons and Alcohol

As Brooke Shields stated for the Will Rogers Institute, White Plains, New York, "The biggest decision a young person makes about alcohol isn't what to drink, it's how to deal with the choices. You can drink moderately, you can let alcohol hurt you, or you can choose not to drink at all. It's up to you. But learn the facts. It's only fair to give yourself a chance to think before you drink."

And Brooke is correct. She recommends reading the Institute's booklet *Teenage Alcohol* which you can obtain free of charge by writing to the Will Rogers Institute at 785 Mamaroneck Avenue, White Plains, NY 10605.

Tip #53
The Ultimate Technique

Whenever you feel pressured to have a drink at a business lunch or dinner, you might remind yourself that in most cases the pressure is more imagined than real. "The old days when you had to drink as part of business are over," says Warren Van Deventer, managing editor of *United States Banker* magazine, in Cos Cob, Connecticut. "People for the most part now are much more concerned about their health, their waistline, and having a clear head."

So when it comes to the point in which you feel a business associate or client is pressuring you to have a drink and you decide to refuse, Van Deventer relays this advice from Bernard Baruch: "Those who mind don't matter, and those who matter don't mind."

Helen Galland, formerly the president of Bonwit Teller and now head of Helen Galland Associates, believes that you have to be honest about your drinking habits. "I like to enjoy myself at a party," she says, "and that means not being intimidated into dreaming up excuses for not having a drink. If I don't want one, that's good enough for me. I just relax and say 'No thank you.'"

Celeste Holm, the renowned stage and screen actress, takes a forthright stand too. "I hate it when people try to force me to have a drink with them. That's not hospitality; it's a violation of it. I don't let them do it."

Gerald Schoenfeld, as chairman of the board of the largest Broadway theater-owning company, The Shubert Organization, is at the top of everyone's guest list. How does he cope with all those drink-ridden opening nights, theater parties, and benefits? "No problem," he says. "When they ask me, I just tell them the truth: 'I don't drink.'"

MAKE A GAME OF IT

Why not make a game of cutting down on your social drinking? The chances are that someone else you know—a friend, business associate, your spouse, your lover—would also like to cut back on his or her social drinking. If you are a successful business person, you probably become more effective when the stakes are higher.

Besides, any kind of new regimen—whether it be a diet, an exercise program, or a drink-reduction program—is easier, more enjoyable, and more durable when you have someone else to participate with. Just as an example: Recreational runners who run in groups of two or more run farther and more often than runners who go it alone. Part of that is competitive—most runners don't like being outclassed even if it is just a training run. But equally important, with the camaraderie and mutual support that is part of doing things together, the discipline seems a lot less rigorous. It's a nice little psychological boost.

If you want to compete head-to-head (or drink-to-drink) with your friends, come up with a fair handicapping system. That's what makes golf such a great game—handicapping allows the duffer to compete on an equal level with Jack Nicklaus. Not everyone drinks an equal amount, of course, so not everyone should have the same handicap.

If you do compete directly with your friends, though, keep it fun. Don't put up a single, outlandishly lavish prize that people will go overboard trying to win. Winning a prize in this kind of competition is obviously less important than making progress toward controlling social drinking. Anyone who makes progress in that direction deserves some kind of commendation.

You don't necessarily have to compete against your friends to bring in a little competitive edge. You can make small wagers with your friends about your own ability to control your consumption. Make a bet that you can keep your drinking under a certain level each month. If you go over, you pay; go under, and you cash in. Professional sports teams often do this sort of thing with those of their athletes who have weight-control problems. They'll fine the athlete when he is over a specified weight at monthly weigh-ins and will pay a bonus when he comes in under the weight.

If nothing else, suggesting some kind of competition among your friends is a nice, subtle way of letting them know you plan to cut back a little on the amount you drink. Even if they choose not to join in, at least they'll know what you're up to when you turn down the extra-drink offer. Suggesting a competition or offering a bet is a nice way of announcing your intention without seeming self-righteous.

A FEW PERSONAL NOTES

Without question, attitudes about drinking are changing. The change is subtle, and in many ways tacit, but it *is* happening. It's comparable, I think, to changing attitudes about smoking.

People today are proud to be nonsmokers. It is an indication that they have a positive attitude about their health. It is a sign of strength and self-discipline. They are obviously in control of their personal habits.

People with control over their social drinking also earn respect for their self-discipline and, in a business atmosphere, their professionalism. People used to regard the person who had a few too many drinks with a kind of tolerant amusement. Laughs and well-wishing would follow him as he stumbled off into the night with a lampshade on his head.

Now the person who drinks too much is regarded with concern at best, and—more likely—annoyance. Among business associates, that person may be seen as sloppy or unreliable—as sure a way as any to short-circuit promotion opportunities.

The age-old, he-man art of "holding one's liquor" is no longer a badge of honor. Instead, people generally take more pride in mastering the art of moderate consumption. Almost everyone I spoke with in preparing this book had become less concerned about the pressures and temptations to drink. A few still felt obliged to have a drink in their hand in certain situations. But more said that they no longer cared if someone might be looking at them askance because they were having soda water instead of Scotch. In fact, they said, you're more likely to earn respect for turning down a drink than for accepting one. And after declining drinks in a few situations, what many found was that the pressure to drink had always been more imagined than real anyway.

Crossing that hurdle was a big step for me. I was from the old school of social drinking, particularly when it came to business lunches. Having two and even three martinis at a business lunch was an accepted part of the modus operandi. Not having a drink or two at lunch seemed as uncouth as wearing an unironed shirt. You looked foolish, and a bit unprofessional. But now I can easily turn down a drink without losing face.

In fact, I've devised a few turn-down lines that I can use whenever I feel someone is pressuring me to have a drink and I really don't want one. (What I've also discovered is that it is the *first* drink offer that carries most of the pressure. If you start with something nonalcoholic, people rarely push you to switch to liquor for your second drink.)

A few of the turn-down lines that work pretty well for me are:

"I'm really thirsty. Do you think I could have a nice big glass of ice water first?"

A Few Personal Notes

"I'm pretty pooped from work, and I think a drink would knock me right out. Do you have any of that great orange juice you usually serve?"

"I think I'd rather wait for the wine with dinner. The wine you serve is always terrific."

You can improvise, of course, but there is no real secret to the effective turn-down line. Say no politely and throw in a compliment at the same time. In most cases, people are more concerned about being properly sociable than they are about whether or not you drink. You can gracefully acknowledge that social gesture without having something to drink.

All this is not to suggest that I've given up drinking entirely. I still enjoy having a drink. In fact, because I am in complete control of my social drinking, I enjoy it more now than I ever did. But I have adopted a new set of rules about my social drinking.

First, I set a curfew for almost all dinner invitations. (For really special occasions, of course, such as a close friend's birthday, I don't want to cut the evening short.) To avoid an uncomfortable encounter, I always let the host know *before* I go. I just say that I'll have to leave at ten-thirty or eleven because I have an important appointment first thing the next morning.

I'm also not afraid to turn down an invitation altogether. If the party is set to start late and I know it's going to be a hard-drinking crowd, I decline right away.

Another important rule I've set for myself is always to plan something to do after any social function that revolves around drinking. If it is an afternoon reception at a club, for example, I make certain to make a reasonably early dinner reservation at a nearby restaurant. That gives me an excuse to offer the person who insists that I stay. And it is the easiest way I know of to keep from lingering at the party and having drinks I don't really want or need.

I classify all my drinks now. I've set up two categories: relaxing drinks and nonsense drinks. Nonsense drinks are those that are thrust upon me (however politely) or drinks, such as nightcaps, that are totally unnecessary. I can't sidestep all those drinks, but I find that it's fairly easy—and usually socially acceptable—to have a glass of fruit juice instead. Relaxing drinks are those I know I'll enjoy—a drink at home with a good friend or an ice-cold beer after a game of tennis. Those are drinks I can savor with immense, slow satisfaction.

And whether they're nonsense drinks or relaxing drinks, I keep an honest count of how much I'm consuming. If I don't, I find it's too easy to let those unwanted drinks slip in.

Finally, I am no longer concerned about what impact my turning down a drink might create—regardless of the occasion. I have reached a point where, when offered a drink, I am completely confident in simply saying, "No thanks."

SEND IN YOUR TIPS

Obviously, my friends, business associates, and other people who have contributed their ideas to this book aren't the only people with methods for keeping down their liquor consumption. Almost everyone I've talked to while putting this book together—at least among people who enjoy having a drink every once in a while—has some little gimmick or strategy to resist having an extra drink.

Oddly enough, people tend to keep those gimmicks and strategies to themselves—I suppose because it is a subject that is so rarely raised. And yet when I asked for contributions for the book, it was as if I had opened a box of jewels. People came forward with great delight to offer their pearls of advice.

I'd like to hear from you too. I am sure that there are some great tips for keeping social drinking under control that have been left out of the book. I've listed just fifty-three in this book—I'm willing to bet that there are literally hundreds of tips that are being used regularly and effectively.

So if you've got a tip for keeping your drinking under control—and it really works for you—send it to me. If it works for you, chances are it will work for someone else. With enough tips, I can help get the word out in a follow-up edition. (You'll find suggestion forms in the back of this book.)

Remember—a drink is to be enjoyed, and you enjoy a drink more when you drink less.

MY DAILY PLAN

Day: 1-2-3-4-5-6-7 (circle one)

Date: _____

OCCASION	NORMAL NUMBER OF DRINKS	TARGET NUMBER OF DRINKS	HOW I MADE OUT	COMMENTS
Lunch	_____	_____	_____	_____
Cocktails	_____	_____	_____	_____
Dinner	_____	_____	_____	_____
Other	_____	_____	_____	_____

Target for day _____

Actual consumption _____

------------------------------------- CUT HERE -------------------------------------

MY DAILY PLAN

Day: 1-2-3-4-5-6-7 (circle one)

Date: _____

OCCASION	NORMAL NUMBER OF DRINKS	TARGET NUMBER OF DRINKS	HOW I MADE OUT	COMMENTS
Lunch	_____	_____	_____	_____
Cocktails	_____	_____	_____	_____
Dinner	_____	_____	_____	_____
Other	_____	_____	_____	_____

Target for day _____

Actual consumption _____

MY DAILY PLAN

Day: 1-2-3-4-5-6-7 (circle one)

Date: _____

OCCASION	NORMAL NUMBER OF DRINKS	TARGET NUMBER OF DRINKS	HOW I MADE OUT	COMMENTS
Lunch	_____	_____	_____	_____
Cocktails	_____	_____	_____	_____
Dinner	_____	_____	_____	_____
Other	_____	_____	_____	_____

Target for day _____

Actual consumption _____

------------------------------------- CUT HERE -------------------------------------

MY DAILY PLAN

Day: 1-2-3-4-5-6-7 (circle one)

Date: _____

OCCASION	NORMAL NUMBER OF DRINKS	TARGET NUMBER OF DRINKS	HOW I MADE OUT	COMMENTS
Lunch	_____	_____	_____	_____
Cocktails	_____	_____	_____	_____
Dinner	_____	_____	_____	_____
Other	_____	_____	_____	_____

Target for day _____

Actual consumption _____

MY DAILY PLAN

Day: 1-2-3-4-5-6-7 (circle one)

Date: _____

OCCASION	NORMAL NUMBER OF DRINKS	TARGET NUMBER OF DRINKS	HOW I MADE OUT	COMMENTS
Lunch	_____	_____	_____	_____
Cocktails	_____	_____	_____	_____
Dinner	_____	_____	_____	_____
Other	_____	_____	_____	_____

Target for day _____

Actual consumption _____

------------------------------------ CUT HERE ------------------------------------

MY DAILY PLAN

Day: 1-2-3-4-5-6-7 (circle one)

Date: _____

OCCASION	NORMAL NUMBER OF DRINKS	TARGET NUMBER OF DRINKS	HOW I MADE OUT	COMMENTS
Lunch	_____	_____	_____	_____
Cocktails	_____	_____	_____	_____
Dinner	_____	_____	_____	_____
Other	_____	_____	_____	_____

Target for day _____

Actual consumption _____

MY WEEKLY PLAN

Week: 1-2-3-4 (circle one)

Date: _____

DAY	NORMAL NUMBER OF DRINKS	TARGET NUMBER OF DRINKS	HOW I MADE OUT
Monday	_____	_____	_____
Tuesday	_____	_____	_____
Wednesday	_____	_____	_____
Thursday	_____	_____	_____
Friday	_____	_____	_____
Saturday	_____	_____	_____
Sunday	_____	_____	_____

Target for week _____

Actual consumption _____

------------------------------ CUT HERE ------------------------------

MY WEEKLY PLAN

Week: 1-2-3-4 (circle one)

Date: _____

DAY	NORMAL NUMBER OF DRINKS	TARGET NUMBER OF DRINKS	HOW I MADE OUT
Monday	_____	_____	_____
Tuesday	_____	_____	_____
Wednesday	_____	_____	_____
Thursday	_____	_____	_____
Friday	_____	_____	_____
Saturday	_____	_____	_____
Sunday	_____	_____	_____

Target for week _____

Actual consumption _____

MY WEEKLY PLAN

Week: 1-2-3-4 (circle one)

Date: _____

DAY	NORMAL NUMBER OF DRINKS	TARGET NUMBER OF DRINKS	HOW I MADE OUT
Monday	_____	_____	_____
Tuesday	_____	_____	_____
Wednesday	_____	_____	_____
Thursday	_____	_____	_____
Friday	_____	_____	_____
Saturday	_____	_____	_____
Sunday	_____	_____	_____

Target for week _____

Actual consumption _____

------------------------------- CUT HERE -------------------------------

MY WEEKLY PLAN

Week: 1-2-3-4 (circle one)

Date: _____

DAY	NORMAL NUMBER OF DRINKS	TARGET NUMBER OF DRINKS	HOW I MADE OUT
Monday	_____	_____	_____
Tuesday	_____	_____	_____
Wednesday	_____	_____	_____
Thursday	_____	_____	_____
Friday	_____	_____	_____
Saturday	_____	_____	_____
Sunday	_____	_____	_____

Target for week _____

Actual consumption _____

MY WEEKLY PLAN

Week: 1-2-3-4 (circle one)

Date: _____

DAY	NORMAL NUMBER OF DRINKS	TARGET NUMBER OF DRINKS	HOW I MADE OUT
Monday	_____	_____	_____
Tuesday	_____	_____	_____
Wednesday	_____	_____	_____
Thursday	_____	_____	_____
Friday	_____	_____	_____
Saturday	_____	_____	_____
Sunday	_____	_____	_____

Target for week _____

Actual consumption _____

------------------------------------ CUT HERE ------------------------------------

MY WEEKLY PLAN

Week: 1-2-3-4 (circle one)

Date: _____

DAY	NORMAL NUMBER OF DRINKS	TARGET NUMBER OF DRINKS	HOW I MADE OUT
Monday	_____	_____	_____
Tuesday	_____	_____	_____
Wednesday	_____	_____	_____
Thursday	_____	_____	_____
Friday	_____	_____	_____
Saturday	_____	_____	_____
Sunday	_____	_____	_____

Target for week _____

Actual consumption _____

MY MONTHLY PLAN

Month: 1-2-3-4-5-6 (circle one)

Date: _____

WEEK	NORMAL NUMBER OF DRINKS	TARGET NUMBER OF DRINKS	HOW I MADE OUT
1st week	_____	_____	_____
2nd week	_____	_____	_____
3rd week	_____	_____	_____
4th week	_____	_____	_____

Target for month _____

Actual consumption _____

---------------------------------- CUT HERE ----------------------------------

MY MONTHLY PLAN

Month: 1-2-3-4-5-6 (circle one)

Date: _____

WEEK	NORMAL NUMBER OF DRINKS	TARGET NUMBER OF DRINKS	HOW I MADE OUT
1st week	_____	_____	_____
2nd week	_____	_____	_____
3rd week	_____	_____	_____
4th week	_____	_____	_____

Target for month _____

Actual consumption _____

MY MONTHLY PLAN

Month: 1-2-3-4-5-6 (circle one)

Date: _____

WEEK	NORMAL NUMBER OF DRINKS	TARGET NUMBER OF DRINKS	HOW I MADE OUT
1st week	_____	_____	_____
2nd week	_____	_____	_____
3rd week	_____	_____	_____
4th week	_____	_____	_____

Target for month _____

Actual consumption _____

------------------------------------ CUT HERE ------------------------------------

MY MONTHLY PLAN

Month: 1-2-3-4-5-6 (circle one)

Date: _____

WEEK	NORMAL NUMBER OF DRINKS	TARGET NUMBER OF DRINKS	HOW I MADE OUT
1st week	_____	_____	_____
2nd week	_____	_____	_____
3rd week	_____	_____	_____
4th week	_____	_____	_____

Target for month _____

Actual consumption _____

MY MONTHLY PLAN

Month: 1-2-3-4-5-6 (circle one)

Date: _____

WEEK	NORMAL NUMBER OF DRINKS	TARGET NUMBER OF DRINKS	HOW I MADE OUT
1st week	_____	_____	_____
2nd week	_____	_____	_____
3rd week	_____	_____	_____
4th week	_____	_____	_____

Target for month _____

Actual consumption _____

------------------------------------- CUT HERE -------------------------------------

MY MONTHLY PLAN

Month: 1-2-3-4-5-6 (circle one)

Date: _____

WEEK	NORMAL NUMBER OF DRINKS	TARGET NUMBER OF DRINKS	HOW I MADE OUT
1st week	_____	_____	_____
2nd week	_____	_____	_____
3rd week	_____	_____	_____
4th week	_____	_____	_____

Target for month _____

Actual consumption _____

To: Richard A. Basini
c/o G. P. Putnam's Sons
200 Madison Avenue
New York, NY 10016

Date: _____

Here is one way I duck drinks I don't really want:

Signed _____

Name and address (capital letters, please) _____

_____

_____

P.S. I have found the following tips in this book particularly useful (cite tips by their numbers):

___ ___ ___ ___ ___ ___ ___
___ ___ ___ ___ ___ ___ ___